# ALTERNATIVE
# EDINBURGH

Clark Kent (alias Superman)
Committed suicide because he failed to find new roles.
The bullets that bounced off him on the screen
Wormed their way in in Real Life.
But who cared for real life?
We had our own world, our own celluloid imaginations
And now we have a different world,
One that's a little more cynical
And we believe, a little more real.
Our Batsignals now questions flung into space
To attract the attention of passing solutions . . . .

**BRIAN PATTEN**

# GREYFRIARS MARKET
# 14 forrest rd

## TEN STALLS SELLING ALMOST ALL YOU'RE LIKELY TO NEED

**ALICE** : all you need in Denim, and that's not all

**BUMBLE:** handmade boots & shoes, unisex clogs

**CAT:** clothes for the fashion conscious girl

**DELTA:** cards, stationery, prints, posters & paper things

**GIFT STALL:** gifts & novelties for the house

**GREYFRIARS EXCHANGE:** buys, sells, exchanges albums & lotsa deletions

**LYN ABBEY:** handmade leatherware—bags, belts, etc.

**MUSIC STALL:** second hand instruments, new accessories, music books bought & sold

**NIRVANA:** a wide range of clothes for both sexes

**SIMPLY SUPER:** period clothes, jewellery, bric a brac

OPEN MON.—SAT.  10 a.m.—6 p.m.

# INTRODUCTION

Whether you're a summer tourist or winter resident, getting to know half a million people takes a lot of socialising. We don't pretend to know everyone or everything that is happening in the City, but in this book we hope to bring together information and views from as many different scenes as possible. The amount of revision needed in the year since the first edition has meant rewriting about half the book, just to keep up with the changes in City politics, community life or even the price of mince.

Yesterday's papers . . .

those predictions we laughed at
in last year's magazine
have become dated —
they've happened.

P.V.B.

"Alternative Edinburgh" is intended to be more than just a guide to Edinburgh. In the limited space available we are attempting to present a synopsis of life in Edinburgh from the housing estates at Craigmillar to the "freak" markets in the City, or a late night rock concert at the Empire.

Last year we produced a book that presented a very harsh and critical view of the city; we were so overwhelmed by the living disasters of Edinburgh that we forgot to mention the good scenes and potentials that make Edinburgh a place to live in, not just an existence.

Many of the best buys in our consumer sections were the result of our own frantic efforts to stave off impending bankruptcy, but just knowing where is the best place to score meat or discount records can save a lot of expensive mistakes. Although this book is intended for the average impoverished "freak about town" (already 50p the poorer) we have included some of the more unique experiences which, despite the outlay of bread involved, have to be tried once.

Our outlook may have changed, so has Edinburgh, but the basic problems haven't. The people are as alienated as ever from the power to shape their own future, limited by the ignorance of the system they're up against, or by lack of alternative living styles. A heavy trip — but persistently true. "Alternative Edinburgh" isn't going to change anything "at a stroke", but we can introduce the situations and possible means of response. You don't have to be political to be aware, or a councillor in order to influence decisions. By using the system's own rules (and a few of your own) you could be surprised by what you can wring out of the establishment.

3

# CONTENTS

# The CREDITS:

'Any connection with any city, living or dead, is purely intentional.'

EDITOR: Barry Wright
GRAPHICS: Johnny Apollo, Dougie Hamilton, John Forsyth
LAYOUT: John Forsyth, Willie Bloch
PHOTOS: Alastair McDougall
TYPESETTING: Bev Ninnes, Sheila Maclean, Audio Type
CONTRIBUTORS: Mike Anderson, Adrian, Tony Aldgate, William Bloch, Gordon Brown, Peter V. Browne, Billy Campbell, Ian Clarkson, Dougie, Major Disaster, John B., Else, Alan Fairlamb, Chrissie Fairlamb, John Forsyth, Gilly Gilmore, Pete Irving, Barry Jones, Sheila Jones, Billy Kay, Pete Lewis, John Leopold, John McGachie, Gus MacLean, Irvine Nagy, Lynea Noble, Ted Ninnes, Bill Olivier, Alan Peden, Margaret Roxton, Captain Starlight, Ron Tuck, July Wilcock, Chris Worsley, Liz Wright, Young Mental Bloch, Ziggy Rector.

Poetry reproduced with thanks to: Alan Jackson (Penguin Modern Poets No. 12), Brian Patten ('Little Johnny's Confession', Geo. Allen & Unwin), Edwin Morgan (Edinburgh University Press), P.V. Browne, Red Mole, C.L.C., Joni Mitchell, Bruce Cockburn, Hugh McDiarmid, Alexander Scott and Brian McCabe.

Also thanks to Audio Type—Mr. Polossi, Scottish Free Radio Assoc., Childrens Rights, BIT, Cracker, Roots, Help, Sandy Ross, Robin Cook, SCCL, WCCL, Social Work Dept., Touch, Tourist Info Office, Scottish Tourist Board, Transport Dept., Meadow Bar.

MIRACLES AND PRINTING by G.P. Management Aids, Ltd.

Published by EUSPB, 1 Buccleuch Pl., Edinburgh
   First edition August '72
   Second edition August '73
Copyright: Barry Wright

**DAS KAPITAL!**

Edinburgh lives and breathes! It's romantic, it's historic, it's beautiful. So be alive to its atmosphere!

You can walk from one end of the city centre to the other in less than one hour, more if you take in the architecture, sights and sounds. Feet will always be in fashion, so use them!

To find your way around the capital, get free maps, guides and brochures especially "Edinburgh and the Lothians" from SCOTTISH TOURIST BOARD, 2 Rutland Place, or TOURIST INFORMATION OFFICE, 1 Cockburn St. (226 6519); open 7 days a week from 09.00—21.00.

The Bus Route map (encased in glass on all bus shelters) is the best map there is, so get your copy, 5p from TRANSPORT HEADQUARTERS, 14 Queen St., or TRANSPORT INFORMATION BUREAU, Waverley Bridge (556 5656).

Edinburgh didn't appear overnight! 1000 years of the diverse human mind has left a deep imprint. Discover for yourself the background of the present city, it's history and culture, by consulting the formidable range of histories and books at the Edinburgh Central and National libraries, situated on George IV Bridge.

Remember this! The map is only a blueprint of the city; to make it come alive, get into it! Here are some routes to help you orientate yourself in the capital.

## OLD EDINBURGH

Begin at the beginning—the Castle—built on volcanic rock and originally fortified by the Picts. It's free to get past the castle gates, but you have to purchase a ticket to see various rooms, e.g. the Crown Jewels. Stand on the ramparts overlooking Princes St.—a total panoramic experience of the city. See where Old and New meet.

From here on in, the capital's heritage unrolls. Move on down the Lawnmarket (the start of the Royal Mile). All the houses are huddled closely together on this stretch because people of old Edinburgh tried to cram as many houses into the city walls as they could for safety and protection. Take a closer look at the Outlook Tower and Canonball House. This high density housing was built in mysterious "closes" and courtyards on both sides of the Royal Mile. Investigate them, it's exciting!

Duck into Milne's Court on a rainy day. Built in 1690, it's the earliest open planning in the Old Town. Don't miss the Ensign Ewart, the pub which celebrates the Waterloo hero who was later denied his war pension, for radical activities, and died a pauper. Drybroughs beer at reasonable prices.

Pass George IV Bridge, and into the High St. Stroll around St. Giles Cathedral, take in the Scottish Law Courts and the old Scottish Parliament House, and back to the High St. Pass the city police HQ. Test your paranoia! Head on down past the Tron and the Bridges; on the right of the High St., a demolition has uncovered a mediaeval Edinburgh bakery and dwelling complex. Peep through the windows on the billboards.

Don't miss out on the Museum of Childhood, well worth the 5p entrance charge. Opposite is the 16th century house of John Knox. Moray House in the Canongate is an old crashpad of Cromwell's. At the foot of the Royal Mile is Holyrood Palace, infamous for Royal garden parties. Crash one, and earn a free copy of A.E. Send two ears for confirmation!

Swing right and climb Arthur's Seat to take in the sunset. What a climb, but what a sight! You can see old and new Edinburgh spread out before you. To round off the trip climb down to Duddingston Loch, cool your feet in the wild bird sanctuary, and drown your thirst in the Sheeps Heid pub in Duddingston Village. When it closes a no. 42 bus will bring you back to the centre.

NEW TOWN

To get the feel of Edinburgh's New Town, start with a view of the city from the top of Edinburgh's Acropolis, Calton Hill, then walk via Waterloo Place, and West Register Street past the Cafe Royal to St. Andrews Square, the Hub of the Scottish money world. Go in and see the ceiling of the Royal Bank of Scotland, remind yourself what capitalism is about.
A walk from St. Andrews Square takes you along George Street, premier Street of the original 'New Town', to Charlotte Square, the North Side, Scotland's Downing Street, is the best preserved example of Adam Architecture around, north to Moray Place, Edinburgh's Belgravia, and down the hill to a very different scene in sunny St. Stephens Street.

TAKE A TRIP TO THE BOTANICS

In the heart of the madding crowd lies an oasis of peace and beauty, the Royal Botanical Gardens, a few minutes walk away from George St. and on the north side.

Walking from the Northern Bar, Canonmills, take in Robert Louis Stevenson's birthplace at No. 8 Howard Place, and enter the Botanics by the east gate. This side is enclosed by the elegant Georgian mansions, protecting the gardens from the city outside. To the right is a shaded pond with mallards, coots and geese who'll appreciate a few scraps, as will the pigeons which follow you from entrance to exit, if you look like a breadwinner!

The new Conservatory is an amazing split level building with steamy Amazon jungles, and arid cactus country under one roof. Look out for the miniature aquarium.

If you survive the man eating creepers, head up the hill towards the Gallery of Modern Art, Inverleith House, a stunning Georgian building.

Before you leave the Botanics explore the Moore and Epstein sculptures on the Art Gallery front lawn. Run your hands over them. Really sensual!

Still feeling speedy? Leave by the west gate and turn south towards the colonies built by the Edinburgh Cooperative Building Society in the 1840's and on to Stockbridge.

At Stockbridge, go past the faded Dean Terrace and up Ann Street, perhaps the most beautiful street in Edinburgh.

Retrace your steps, cross the river and take the footpath to Dean Village along the left bank of the river. The posh private back gardens of elegant Georgian Moray and Ainslie Places run down to the footpath where the shade of the overhanging boughs and the whispering river gives a feeling of serenity. Suddenly, you're at St. Bernards Well, a Grecian style temple on the site of the old 18th century spa. On under Thomas Telford's Dean Bridge completed in 1832, and into Dean Village, once a thriving mill community supplying Edinburgh with flour. A casualty of the Industrial Revolution, it is now being renovated as housing.

Leave the Village by Bell's Brae and back to the hubbub of the west end, where in Rose Street the pubs may just be opening.

## TOURS WITH PERKS

Walking around Edinburgh, absorbing the historical and architectural magnificence doesn't fill an empty stomach or slake a thirst. It's time to start trucking on a tour round the brewers and bakers, but remember that they will only be interested in organised parties, so find some friends. Ask for a tour, mentioning your fascination in breweries but don't worry about the conversation, they know why you're there. Edinburgh is Britain's second largest brewing centre which means that a little planning when you organise the tours (preferably a week's notice) should give you a full day's heavy boozing.

A sample of the possibilities:

The Tennent Caledonian brewery at Roseburn (667 3311) in the morning,St. Leonards St. brewery (667 3511) in the afternoon, and finally down hill to the Scottish and New-castle breweries in Holyrood Rd. (556 2591). If your mind or stomach turns to food get into one of the many bakeries around Edinburgh. Begin with Milanda (448 6041) and Burtons (443 5281) on the Sighthill Industrial Estate; they have more than enough biscuits to accommo-date your simple desires. For more ideas look up the Yel-low Pages.

## THE BEGINNING OF THE GRAPEVINE

It may be easy to get the feel of the city by walking round but you'll still be a "tourist" till you meet the natives.

To find friends, parties, a crashpad or a flat, the best way is to get in on the grapevine. Many of the freak scenes revolve around only a handful of pubs. Try St. Vincents, the mecca for Stockbridge freaks, Cafe Royal and Abbots-ford in Rose St., or Bennets, Tollcross where workers, actors, straights and freaks rub shoulders.

During University term time, the Student Centre, Bristo St., H.W.S.U., Grindlay St. and the Meadow Bar, Buccleuch St. should be added to your list. If you dig folksinging, Sandy Bells is a must, or if left wing politics and poets are your fancy, Milnes Bar in Hanover St.

During the day a walk round Headquarters, S. College St., Greyfriars and Cockburn St. Markets and Jenny Wright's in Lauriston Place (don't trip over Rug) will yield amazing finds in goodies and friends. Alternatively explore St. Stephen St., Stockbridge and stop in for a meal in Mother Earth.

If you're into theatre, the Pool and the Traverse are where the cognescenti hang out. Traverse membership is also useful for late night meals and Sunday drinking. But this is only the beginning, for more clues, read on!

aye it's REAL EDINBURGH.

A full 'official' tour round Edinburgh's beauty spots costs £1: you can see the real Edinburgh — the best and worst — for only 9p on the 2/12 Corporation bus, boarded at Nicholson Sq., at Haymarket, in the Grassmarket — or better in South St. Andrews St.

You will find that Edinburgh offers the reverse of Galbraith's dictum: it has public affluence and private squalor, the other side to the image sedulously fostered by generations of Lord Provosts, tourist promoters and brochure writers. The city offers a prime example of co-exploitation: the shopkeeper, hotelier, restauranteur, and conference organiser exploits the tourist; the city's resources are pumped into beautifying the centre and its tourist-cultural attractions; and the tourist and middle-class resident exploits the worker who is pushed miles out into the outskirts — Pilton, Craigmillar, Wester Hailes and Broomhouse — without even the meagrest of amenities or left in the concealed slums of the centre of nineteenth century tenements of Leith. In July the floral clock is replanted and the Grassmarket regulars are moved on.

The International Festival, like the best of Edinburgh, is great — apart from the fact that most of Edinburgh's people cannot afford it. 'Cracker' in a recent poll found that only 27% of their sample attended anything at all at last year's festival. There is little of Edinburgh — less of Scotland — in the Festival and that is why the alternatives, the Craigmillar Festival in June and the Leith Festival in August every year, have emerged. Both are as far as possible free — the people are fighting back.


## THE GREAT CIRCLE ROUTE

The 2/12 bus is the most comprehensive bus in the city, cost 9p (kids 3p) for the two-hour journey round the best and worst of Edinburgh. The 2/12 can be boarded at South St. Andrews St. (12), the Scott Monument, the West End, Haymarket, but you can also take it from the Grassmarket, Leith Walk or Nicholson Sq. Don't expect to see industry on your tour — look for government buildings, the biggest employer of labour in this tourist-orientated city.

**PRINCES STREET:** Tourist facade of Edinburgh. On left, Scott Monument, Castle and Gardens, on right, shopping area.

**HAYMARKET:** past traffic abomination to first generation railway station (1842), still threatened by Norwich Union Office block development and link road plans.

**ROSEBURN AND MURRAYFIELD'.** Past ice rink, on right Donaldson's School — a Victorian heritage — on left one of city's breweries. Edinburgh is the second largest brewing centre in Britain. You are entering bourgeois Edinburgh, Murrayfield Ground on left and a good view of the Pentlands.

**BOURGEOIS—LIBERAL CORSTORPHINE:** past literally crowded zoo to rows of houses and secluded gardens. Low cost shopping centres, seventy-five shops in main street and innumerable open areas. Barnton can be reached by turning right.

**BROOMHOUSE:** to the right Sighthill Industrial Estate — one of only two industrial blocks in city. On the left Broomhouse, a 1945-50 council estate separated from privately owned houses by railway. Estate used to house problem families. On right white government buildings. In Stevenson Drive — Edinburgh's attempt at a community centre.

**GORGIE/DALRY:** Through towards Dalry — 1880's houses, now the highest proportion of sub-standard houses per ward in city. Open waste ground on left and right, overgrown cemetery on right as you enter Dalry Rd.

**HAYMARKET, MORRISON STREET, BREAD STREET:** Through shops and tenements towards Grassmarket. On left Government buildings, especially the Dept. of Social Security — and new G.P.O. Headquarters and above you on the left the Castle Barracks and down the hill the Grassmarket.

**GRASSMARKET:** most studied area in Scotland. Centre for city's drifting population. The two faces of exploitation: the businesses, dealers and entertainments who want tenants and winos moved out, and Castle Trades and Greyfriars Hotel, £2.10 weekly, 6 x 5 x 7 ft. cubicle. 625 beds in area. Big profits. Roots have recently highlighted the conditions in the hostels and can give more information, if interested. On right in the Vennel, Salvation Army's Women's Hostel where homeless families are broken up, and Heriot Watt University. To the east, the Cowgate, the Church's shelter for winos banned from lodging houses. In summer, down and outs are moved on for the tourists — prosecutions, for loitering, begging and drunkenness increase.

**TOP OF CANDLEMAKER ROW:** on near left statue of 'Greyfriars Bobby' (originally a fountain for dogs — typically perhaps water cut off in '55); on right, pub of same name — no dogs allowed. On far left George IV Bridge. National Library and Royal Mile. On towards University and waste ground as University with council connivance takes over housing space, moves people out and builds architectural monstrosities.

**THE PLEASANCE:** Awaiting demolition for the building of a six-lane Eastern Link Road. On the far left Salisbury Crags, below it new houses soon to be isolated by motorway.

**PRESTONFIELD:** Bourgeois Edinburgh again after one passes Commonwealth Pool and University's residences at Pollock Halls. Through Prestonfield Estate to Prestonfield and several hundred yards of open space.

**CRAIGMILLAR:** Main Road through 1930's estate, sadly lacking in amenities: no launderette, electricity or gas office, coffee bars or cinema and for 30,000 people less than 30 shops. A community centre is only now being built because of efforts of 'Craigmillar Festival Committee, the biggest of the community action groups. who run yearly free festival and playgroups/workshops/stimulate groups. Through Niddrie notice the shops barred up at night.

**NIDDRIE ROAD:** Jewel cottages, ex miners cottages on left and right, some nearest the road deserted, others behind them still occupied. See also Newcraighall, where a dying mining community is being resurrected by the effort of its tenants Assoc., Miners Welfare Club and Councillor David Brown.

PORTOBELLO: Through suburbia to Portobello High St., open air pool dwarfed by cathedral-like Portobello Power Station and fumes from its badly designed chimneys.

SEAFIELD: Round Craigentinny past sewage works to Seafield Rd. East, affluent to effluent, where pollution confronts you on shore. Leave windows open to fully appreciate spectacle. Ahead Leith docks area, and see also site of new sewage partial treatment plant on reclaimed land by shore.

LEITH: Foot of Leith Walk. On right new shopping centre ahead road to Pilton and on left Leith Walk, from where you can see much of condemned Edinburgh; slum tenements and waste ground off the side streets. Past Borders Bar the pre-1914 border between Leith and Edinburgh.

YORK PLACE: From ignored Edinburgh into tourist Edinburgh, with the New Town and Georgian architecture ahead and to the right. On the first right, Broughton Street where Georgian houses are threatened with demolition and above you St. James Sq., hideous commercial development of stores, hotels and ironically, the Ministry of the Environment.

If you want to expand your tour from comprehensive to near complete, the 32 bus — Leith Shore, Pilton, Granton, Sighthill and Wester Hailes — is a worthwhile journey. For this pick up a 32 at the foot of Leith Walk and rejoin the 2/12 at Broomhouse.


## SIX OTHER SIGHTS

If you've just come to Edinburgh you've got to see the Castle, the Palace, Princes Street, the New Town and Cramond. As a contrasting experience five other sights— Castle Barracks, Duddingston Flats (reached by 42 bus), Tennant St., Leith, Pennywell Rd., Pilton and Leith Fort make up a city which few people who live here have fully seen. If you've got time look also at Leith Dockland and Danube St. (declining aristocracy mingling until recently with the prostitution trade).


### HOMELESSNESS/CASTLE BARRACKS/DUDDINGSTON FLATS

Two persons live in the Castle: twenty-one families have space in the Castle Barracks facing it. The army moved out in the Fifties and condemned them as unfit for human habitation: six years later the Corporation opened it as a reception centre for homeless families and two hundred people moved in. An official report, 'Home-

lessness' (1972) spoke of mice, damp, dirt with no good refuse disposal and a complete lack of playing facilites for over 100 kids, hence the recent playground project. Homeless families were also moved into the Salvation Army's Women's Hostel in the Vennel, the west side of the Grassmarket, which accommodates old ladies and young girls off the street. The family is split up and fathers visit between 18.00 and 22.00.

Homeless families can end up for a year in Duddingston Flats. Looking round, you will discover fifty-seven families, most eating, living and sleeping in one room with the barest of furniture.

Homelessness occurs mainly because of rent arrears — Edinburgh's eviction rate is Scotland's highest with fourteen out of every hundred kids in care, homeless because of evictions. 'Homelessness' concluded that "temporary accommodation in Edinburgh was based on a principle more related to retribution, the physical condition being crude and uncomfortable, and the amount of intensive care and support negligible".


## SLUMS/TENNANT STREET, LEITH

Take a 35 bus to Bonnington Rd. Alternatively go to the foot of Leith Walk, turn left and cut back to the right. Off Bonnington Rd. are Edinburgh's worst slum conditions, mainly privately owned and under condemned orders for the last five years. In Tennant Street people live in houses with no windows, and in buildings registered as unsafe. You will find similar conditions in Bollington Street, Bangor St., West Bowling Green St., and others. Many tenements lie empty

17

waiting to be pulled down. The Corporation has no alternative accommodation for people in Leith and wants to use the space for industry. In Gorgie-Dalry the situation is little better. The Jones survey (1968) found 28,000 unfit amenity deficient houses in the city, three times the Scottish national average. One in four houses had no hot water: one in six no bath; and one in fifteen shared WC.

## DEPRIVATION/PILTON ESTATE

### 'This wifie'

This wifie wi a shoppin basket,
A goes up tae her an says
Hey wifie, see, there's the wild Pentlands
Just behind ye.
She d$_{ra}$$_{pp}$$_{ed}$ it.

### ALAN JACKSON

You can travel through Pilton on a 32 bus — you can even stay there. We counted one hundred boarded up houses in West Pilton alone. A recent report of Pilton Central Association found Pilton

leading in incidence of suicide and self-poisoning. Infectious diseases are 20.2 per 1000 (the Edinburgh average is 9.17). Social deprivation is endemic to Pilton, concluded the report: backcourts are overgrown and strewn with glass. There is only one cafe and one snack bar for 50,000 people. The so-called gang problem — Young Muirhouse Team, Young Pilton Derry, Mental Drylaw — represents in reality groups of youngsters attempting to create a meaningful community life. Similar conditions exist at Craigmillar, Sighthill, Broomhouse, and Wester Hailes, the city's newest slum. For years the council has vacillated over building community centres, costing less than £100,000: sports facilities for the Commonwealth Games cost £5m. The Opera House will cost over £10m.

## PLANNING/LEITH FORT

In 1958, Leith Fort — housing one thousand people — won an architectural award; in 1972 a Leith Community Association was "appalled by the starkness and drabness which perpetuates the atmosphere of barracks". Nine out of ten residents questioned found inadequate facilities and it's not difficult to appreciate the uncanny resemblance to the Cancelot Mills across the road. The Fort, reached by a No. 1 or 32 bus, is only one example of the Corporation building slums for the future. In recent years Edinburgh

has produced Britain's best architects: their offices, like the University Town and Planning Department are all in Georgian Edinburgh.

They took all the trees
And put them in a tree museum
And they charged all the people
A dollar and a half just to see 'em

Put away that D.D.T. now
Give me spots on my apples
But leave me the birds and the bees
Please!

# POLLUTION!

## THE FILTH OF FORTH

### THE ESTUARY

The Forth is dirty. Though our area is highly industrialised by far the biggest polluters are human beings, indeed, it's us the citizens of Edinburgh, who are the greatest culprits.

Edinburgh is like an old lady who fastidiously powders her nose but forgets to wipe her backside. Edinburgh's backside as local residents well know is around Seafield, (where eight outfalls belch 24 million gallons of crude sewage onto the Edinburgh seafront every day and where for most of the year, oxygen levels sink below the point of critical sufficiency for supporting sea life.

Edinburgh's solution is a typical half measure. More interested in short term political gain and keeping down the rates, the Council have opted for a partial treatment sewage plant costing £18 million, which will do little more than chop up the sewage and pump it through one pipe, instead of 8.

Already some experts fear that natural changes in the sea-bed and tidal currents at Seafield, could mean that the discharge in the future will be brought back on the shore making pollution even more pronounced than at present. A walk from Cramond to Granton or Seafield to Portobello along the shore should be enough to convince any citizen

21

that the £25 million required for a full treatment plant would be money well spent.

Up river from Edinburgh the inner Forth is spoiled by grease, oil, faeces and bumph on many of the would-be pleasure beaches. From Kincardine up to Alloa their is often critical oxygen deficiencies in the water between March and July (depending on the state of tides and rainfall). Upstream at Stirling technical problems are holding up construction of a sewage treatment plant which at earliest will come into operation around 1976.

Going seawards from Edinburgh the pollution is mainly treated, however, their are certain black spots on the Fife shore. At East Wemyss, N.C.B. workings have resulted in a discharge of iron on the shore. Amounts up to 15 tons/day and an ochrous stain in the estuary up to ½ mile long and several hundred yards wide, has been recorded. At Leven there is a considerable discharge of sewage from inland towns together with distillation liquor from the gas works at Westfield.

## RIVER RUNDOWN

The Rivers of the Forth system vary from fairly clean to gunge-laden cesspools. Fish content can be taken as a fair guide to the river's condition.

FORTH — In its freshwater reaches this river holds a good head of coarse fish and the odd, albeit foolhardy, salmon ventures up soupy waters contaminated by agricultural drains and seepages.

LEVEN — A sewer going down the watercourse alleviates the worst pollution, but occasional leakages of gas distillation liquors wipe out any fish.

CARRON — In its lower reaches this river bears resemblance to the bog at Easter Road, suffering from bad industrial pollution mainly from paper mills.

AVON — is conspicuous for its magnificent variety of colours. Although usually a delicate pastel cream it can flow Sunset Orange or blood red, not due to industrial disputes further upstream, but due to paper mills dyeing their products. The bed of this river, like the Carron, is choked with paper fibres making aquatic life impossible. The argument, needless to say, is that the costs of eliminating this pollution would threaten the men's jobs in the mills.

ALMOND — Has improved greatly in last decade since its days as an open sewer and though the fish ladder at Cramond has been unsuccessful, occasional salmon get upstream.

**WATER OF LEITH** — Again a piped sewer down the water course has improved the river and now good trout fishing can be had even in the centre of the city.

**ESK** — has improved recently due to the closure of several mills and the remaining one being compelled to treat its effluent.

**TYNE** — thanks to the efforts of the East Lothian Purification Board in building sewage treatment plants this river now has a fine stock of trout and seatrout.

## AIR POLLUTION

Edinburgh was supposed to be smokeless by 1975 but considerable areas of the city remain unrestricted, and now even the new target date of 1982 is unlikely. Air pollution is exacerbated by two principal industrial polluters, SAI Chemicals in Leith where the yellow fumes have decimated trees and led to local petitions and secondly, Portobello Power Station where the badly designed dynamics of the chimney, with its 80 ft. wide neck mean that the fumes spill over the lip and fall on the houses and swimming pool below. (See also 'Wheels and Deals').

## DOMESTIC RUBBISH

90% of domestic rubbish is still tipped into old quarries or used to reclaim land, but manufacturers' love affair with packaging and with plastic in particular has overloaded this inadequate system as Hailes Quarry bears witness. Individual action may seem futile, but as your gesture start refusing unnecessary packaging and avoiding non-biodegradable packaging and if there's enough customer resistance things might change.

## LOCAL GROUPS

Ecology is one of the major issues facing us today but the ecological groups range from the specific (anti-fluoridisation anti-motor car) to those with general environmental concerns and if you're fussy about political bedfellows, a word of caution, the cause of ecology is as highly favoured by the extreme right as by the left, so beware learned professors advocating taxes on children, etc.

**FRIENDS OF THE EARTH, 19 DUNDAS ST., Tel: 031-556 1872** — local working groups on recycling, overpackaging, population, sewage disposal, Water of Leith, transport, North Sea Oil.

**EDGE** — Environmental Design Group, Edinburgh, 39 Palmerston Place, Edinburgh. — The society for students in Heriot-Watt Town and Country Planning Unit — hold social and academic events and an annual magazine Zoo.

SOCIETY FOR SOCIAL RESPONSIBILITY IN SCIENCE — J. Bate, 1 Warrender Park Cres., Edin. EH9 1DX, Tel: 031-229 7123. The name tells all.

SCIENCE FOR PEOPLE, Flat 2F1, 171 Dalkeith Road, Edin. Tel: 031-667 3482. — Concerned with sciences' interaction with society and its misuse. Particularly interested in local pollution, alternative technology and education.

CONSERVATION SOCIETY, c/o Arthur Bennett, 3 Links Place, Edinburgh, EH6 7EZ. Tel: 031-554 3059 — believes world is unable to support increasing population at present living standards and calls for a reduction in birth rate and more.

EDINBURGH PURE WATER ASSOCIATION — Raymond Reid, 7 Albyn Place, Edinburgh, Tel: 031-337 4381. — opposed to fluoridisation of the city's water supply.

NATIONAL TRUST FOR SCOTLAND, 5 Charlotte Sq., Edinburgh, Tel: 031-225 2184.

# NATIONAL ORGANISATIONS WITHOUT EDINBURGH CONTACTS

CENTRAL COUNCIL FOR RIVERS PROTECTION, Fishmongers Hall, London, E.C.4. Tel: 01-626 3531.

COASTAL ANTI-POLLUTION LEAGUE, Alverstoke, Greenway-lane, Bath, Somerset.

NATIONAL SOCIETY FOR CLEAN AIR, 136 North St., Brighton, BN1 1RG, Tel: 0273-26313.

NOISE ABATEMENT SOCIETY, 6 Old Bond Street, London, W.1. Tel: 01-493 5877.

POPULATION STABILIZATION, 6 St. Marks Place, London, W.11, Tel: 01-229 8249.

POSITIVE MOVEMENT, 10 Lady Somerset Rd., Kentish Town, London, NW5 1NS. Tel: 01-485 1646.  "nice one".

RAMBLERS ASSOCIATION, 1-4 Crawford Mews, York Street, London, W.1.

ROYAL SOCIETY FOR THE PROTECTION OF BIRDS, The Lodge, Sandy, Beds. Tel: 076-78551.

SOIL ASSOCIATION, Walnut Tree Manor, Haughley, Stowmarket, Suffolk.

# MAGAZINES

THE ECOLOGIST, 73 Molesworth St., Wadebridge, Cornwall. Tel: Wadebridge 2296/7. 'The' magazine on ecology, but accused of having suspect political connections.

TOWARDS SURVIVAL, 79 Sutton Ave., Eastern Green, Coventry. 0203-463062. — a monthly journal on ecology.

ROOTS—leave messages temporarily with HELP, 554 6098, while Roots are changing address.   Community monthly with an ecological heart.

# EATING.

best
beans ken

Y ou have to eat to survive but if possible eating should also
be fun. The sensual delights of a good meal make it all
worthwhile. Edinburgh is well endowed with eating
places. This is a selection of recommended restaurants.

## CHEAP

Most ostensibly cheap restaurant chains are more interested
in profit margins than good food, so as a general rule avoid
them. If you can afford only around 25p and little more
for a meal, recommended restaurants for cheapness (not
necessarily attractive) and value are the following:

THE ARTISAN, Grove St. (5 mins. From Haymarket. Working
men's hostel. Cheapest place in town, filling but... Breakfasts
(bacon and egg) served from 05.00 (Sun. 06.00).

THE MUSEUM TEAROOM, Chambers St. (entry from Lothian St.).
Pies, salads; limited range. 11.00—16.00 (excl. Sundays).

YMCA CAFE, 14 St. Andrew St. Main lunch course choice includes fish, stew or gammon steak. 0900—21.30 (excl. Sundays).

YWCA CAFETERIA, 7 Randolph Pl., breakfast, lunch, high tea and
coffee from 09.30—18.00 (Sat. 09.30—14.00),closed Suns. Main
dishes salads and meats.

UNION SNACK BAR, 18 Union Pl. 07.00—18.00. 3-course lunch,
cheap.

PURPLE SQUARE, 42 West Preston St. (nr. Meadows). Omelettes,
casseroles. 09.00—20.00 (excl. Sun.). Clean.

THE POP INN, 491 Lawnmarket. 09.00—18.30. Best value of

Royal Mile cafes.

THE DRUMMOND, 9 Drummond St. Nice shepherds pie. Similar value next door at CAFE, 11 Drummond St.

BAMBI, 66 South Bridge. Highly recommended. Nice food.

THE WEE SNACK BAR, 227 Leith Walk. Salads reasonable, range not extensive.

THE GRIDDLE, 187 Leith Walk. 3-course lunches.

TAM'S SNACK BAR, West Nicholson St. 09.00—17.00. Cheap. Lunches—steak pie, veg. and potatoes a bargain.

THE QUICK AND PLENTY, 27 Leven St. Bacon, sausage, egg, tomatoes at 06.30 (for breakfast)—17.00.

LEITH DOCKS TRANSPORT CAFE (outside main dock gate). Enough said.

NEW ATHOLL, 3 Atholl Pl. 09.00—15.00. Salads good. Carry-out service ;

## FISH AND CHIP SHOPS

If you want to eat fillingly and cheaply, fish and chip shops are a good buy with prices for pie and chips ranging from 15p upwards. You can find a fish shop at almost every second street corner—some have sit-down meals and are open at lunchtime. The best for quality and access are:

QUO VADIS, 145 Dalry Rd. Lunch served 11.30 to 14.30 at 35p. Superb range of dishes, open till 23.00

THE INTERNATIONAL, 169—175 Gilmore Pl., 11.30—14.30, 16.30—24.00.

JPE'S FRITTER BAR, West Nicolson St. 15—30p for sit-down or takeaway dishes.

HARRY'S FISH BAR, 79 Brougham St. Opens 17.00 but sit-down meals. Known to give away free pies at midnight.

THE GLOBETROTTER, 169 Bruntsfield Pl. Very clean. Open 11.30—13.30, 17.00—23.00

BRATTISANIS, 25 Brougham Pl. and 2 Henderson Row (midday to 23.30); 87 Newington Rd., 272 Morrison St. (09.30—23.30) and Raeburn Pl. (midday to 14.00, 16.30—23.30).

## CARRY-OUT

Another alternative to restaurants is 'carry out' food. Now even more attractive because it is exempt from VAT. There are several excellent carry out shops in town. Most bakers sell hot pies, bridies and rolls for carrying out, and a trip to a delicatessen can yield a delicious picnic.

A few suggested carry out shops:

ANDERSON 'S BAKERIES, 5 West Nicolson St., others in food section.

CAUSEWAYSIDE BAKERIES, Causewayside.

THISTLE DAIRY, 60 Thistle St.   Popular with office staff.
DUNCAN'S, 38 Buccleuch St.
ARNOTTS—Delicatessen, South Bridge.
DELICACIES CENTRE, Barony St., off Broughton St.
CONNOISSEURS, Lochrin Buildings, Tollcross.
VALVONA DELICATESSEN, 19 Elm Row.  Carry-out pizzas from 15p.
ITALIAN BAKERS, 49 Elm Row.  Italian chicken specialities, 12p and 15p upwards.
YUMMIE DOOS, 184 Rose St.  Nice baked potatoes, etc.
MR. CHUKITYLEAF, 12 Barclay Terr.  Expensive but OK for a change.  Filled baked potatoes.
MR. CHIPS, Rose St.
THE POTATO WAGON, 6 Newington Rd.

Indian and Chinese restaurants will also oblige.

## STUDENT RESTAURANTS

University and College student refectories are a good bet for cheap meals, because there are usually few enforceable restrictions on entry.   If challenged just say you've forgotten your student card.

The ones in the centre are:

HERIOT WATT, 30 Grindlay St., 11.45—13.45, 16.45—18.30 all year.
EDINBURGH UNIVERSITY STUDENT CENTRE, Bristo St., open 09.00—20.00 (in term).  Open to 14.00 in vacation.
DAVID HUME TOWER CAFETERIA, George Sq., easy to enter. 09.00—17.00 (only during university term).
ART COLLEGE CANTEEN, Lauriston Pl.—in term 12.15—13.45, 15.30—16.30, 22.30—23.30.  Also college club, Lauriston Pl., 16.00—21.00

## CANTEENS

Finally it is possible, if you've got the nerve and are suitably dressed for the part to eat in the staff canteens of big organisations. Ones we've tested for easy entry and cheapness are:

GPO, 149 Rose St. (opp. Rose and Crown).  08.30—16.00.
LOTHIAN HOUSE, Lothian Rd.  2 courses 20p.
CIVIL SERVICE, St. Andrews House and Jeffrey St. (top floor). 2 courses 20p.
SCOTTISH AND NEWCASTLE BREWERIES, Holyrood Rd. Its 190 Fountainbridge counterpart is more difficult to penetrate (follow crowds to lift at 12.30).  Scampi or rabbit and veg. 10p.
LEITH DOCKS TRANSPORT CAFE.  Meal for 15—20p.  Open to all.

The threat of a freak invasion, after our first edition recommendations, made the BANK OF SCOTLAND, the Mound, tighten its security checks (it's amazing who reads this book), but restrictions are difficult to enforce and soon abandoned.

## COFFEE AND SNACKS

While most restaurants serve coffee and snacks, there are also a few nice places which specialise in a civilised snack. A few of our favourites:

THE DUBLINERS, 29 Dublin St.—attractive whitewashed basement.
CIRCA 1800, 8 Deanhaugh St. Coffee and antiques.
THE LAIRD'S LARDER, 36 Victoria St. 17th century wallpaper and home-made cakes.
THE GRAIL BOOK & ARTS CENTRE, 36 George St., selling excellent coffee and filled rolls among a good selection of books and craft gifts.

**cocoa**

making love to you
was like
drinking cold milk
from a warm glass

i wanted cocoa

BRIAN McCABE

## LUNCH

Since most workers and tourists haven't the time to prepare or scout around for a midday meal a thriving industry has built up around the formula lunch, designed supposedly to cut overheads by limiting your choice of dishes. Many otherwise expensive restaurants offer standard two or three course lunches at around 40—50p per head:

ITALIAN: SORRENTO, 15 Albert Pl., CAPRICE, Leith Walk. INDIAN: ROYAL BENGAL, 4 Forrest Road, CURRY HOUSE, 14 West Nicolson St. CHINESE: CHINA GARDEN, 28 South Clerk St., HUNG LAM, 96 South Clerk St., THE DIAMOND, 44 Grindlay St., the SILVER BOWL, Leith Walk. GENERAL: CRANFORD RESTAURANT, 22 Clerk St., HOPETOUN, 18 Morrison St., KENYA RESTAURANT, 8 Lauriston Pl., DE VITTO, 215 Leith Walk, DIGEST, 19 Dundas St., THE GRADUATE, 17 Forrest Rd., EDINBURGH RENDEZVOUS, 10a Queensferry St., THE EASTERN SEA, 14 Home St.


## PUBS

Pubs are not cheap places to score a lunch, especially after a few pints to wash it all down, but some of the best we found for value were:

McGUFFIES TAVERN, 15 Market St. 2 course lunch including, for example, fish or braised steak. Popular with railwaymen and journalists.

ABBOTSFORD, 3 Rose St. Salmon, scampi and steak in menu with the sausages, egg etc.

BENNETS, 8 Leven St. (next to Kings Theatre). Main courses casseroles, chicken curries. Home made soup excellent.

MILNES, Hanover St. Hot dishes, salads and curries. No desserts but carry-out soup.

ROYAL GEORGE, King George IV Bridge (next to National Library).

WINDSOR BUFFET, 45 Elm Row (next Gateway Theatre). Salads, extensive main dishes. Not cheap but good value.

THE PEACOCK, Main St., Newhaven. Soup and main courses. Specialities include fish dishes from the local catch at lunchtime and teatime.

THE IMPERIAL BAR, The Shore, Leith. Men only in fine dark brown pub in out of way spot. Sit down lunches popular with dockers and businessmen, good value.

THE MORTAR, Forrest Rd. Salads, baked potatoes and usually a hot meal. Good choice of cheap food but dear booze.

# RESTAURANTS FOR THE EPICUREAN

## ITALIAN

COSMO'S, 58 Castle St. (225 6743). You should book for the best Italian in town but don't expect to pay less than £1.50. Otherwise try good Italian food at the SORRENTO, 15 Albert Pl., the PALUMBO, 40 Bruntsfield Pl. and LA COSTIERA, 42 Leven St.

## INDIAN

There are no really first class Indian restaurants in Edinburgh but the ROYAL BENGAL, Forrest Rd. and BABAR'S, Brougham Pl., are worthwhile though pricey. The EURASIAN, Buccleuch St. is also nice, but not cheap. On the cheaper side (around 60p) are the PUNJAB, 45 St. Patrick Sq. and the LOTHIAN Restaurant, Drummond St.

## CHINESE

The LOON FUNG, 2 Warriston Pl. and the WELL MET at the corner of Leamington Terr. and Gilmore Pl., Cantonese restaurants, are the numbers one and two Chinese in Edinburgh. Other Chinese restauranteurs make it round to them when they're closed, which is recommendation enough. Open till 02.00 and average cost about £1. The SIK TEK FOK, Hanover St., rates third of the three Cantonese, also open till 02.00. The EDINBURGH RENDEZVOUS, 10a Queensferry Rd. is Edinburgh's only Pekingese restaurant, good prices, around £1/head. Of the Chop Suey joints the best value we know are the HUNG LAM, Morningside Rd. and S. Clerk St., the HOUSE OF CHOI, Bruntsfield Pl. and the CASTLE, Royal Mile. Prices around 75p/head.

## FRENCH

L'ETOILE, 8a Grindlay St. is a small friendly French restaurant. Positively the best in town, escargots and steaks are specialities. But expensive—expect over £2/head—a favourite for blow-out meals. LE CAVEAU, Hanover St., is a wine bar and restaurant run by the L'Etoile people, almost as good and slightly cheaper.

## GOURMET

More traditional European cuisine restaurants—mainly French. These are good but tend to be expensive and formal.

HAWES INN, South Queensferry—beautiful inn on unique site. £2—3/head.

HANSEL, Stafford St.—good but formal. £2.

CAFE ROYAL, W. Register St.—imperial decadence—real style. £2.

CRAMOND INN, Cramond—another old inn, specialities lobster, salmon, pheasant and rough pate. £2.

BEEHIVE, Grassmarket—speciality steaks. £2.

DANNY BROWNS, George St.—intimate basement—£2.

HOUSESHOE, Eddleston, steaks almost worth 20 mile trip. £1.50.

PERIGORD, George Hotel. Cold table—all you can eat for fixed price.

DORIC TAVERN—Doric steaks and the proprietor Jimmy McGuffie are the specialities of the house. £1.50.

## AMERICAN

NEW YORK STEAM PACKET, first US steak **house** in Edinburgh. Steaks, hamburgers, banana cream pie, blueberry and pineapple cheesecake, nice music and happy faces. £1.50, cheaper for lunch.

KING HERO—Hero sandwiches and steaks and hamburgers. Slightly cheaper than NYSP.

## THEATRE RESTAURANTS

POOL and TRAVERSE, good medium price, nice way to complete the theatre trip.

## OTHERS

SWISS: DENZLERS, very typically Swiss catering, very nice small dining room for parties up to 12 people. £1/head lunch, £1.50 evening.

SPANISH: CASA ESPANOLA—if you must have Spanish fare this is the only place.

SICILIAN: CASA SICILIANA is the only one of that ilk.

SCANDINAVIAN: HOWGATE INN, Howgate, nr. Penicuik—our favourite smorgasbord; NORSEMAN, Norway House, Shandwick Pl.—same style; ALBYN—also has smorgasbord.

## HEALTH FOODS/VEGETARIAN

According to one of Edinburgh's unrecognised sages, George Scott Williamson, "Health = the faculty for mutual synthesis between an organisation and its environment", and even on a very basic level there are few enough shops and restaurants which fill the bill, and they're not necessarily 'health' gigs. We liked the first few; the rest just happen to be there.

HENDERSONS SALAD TABLE, Hanover St.—when they're good they're very good, when they're bad try MOTHER EARTH (below). Going through a new lease of life with the opening of their wine bar extension. Try one of their hot dishes, e.g. stuffed marrows. They can afford to be surly—there's always a queue. Also have bar adjoining on Thistle Street, greengrocery on street level where veg. but not fruit are organically cultivated, and bakery further down on Brandon Terr., Canonmills.

THE LAIGH, Hanover St. So this is what an 18th century coffee house was like. Salads and hot dishes, own blend of coffee, delicious cakes and gateaux baked in their own bakery further down the street, even a newspaper rack. It if's too crowded go to their basement for a more informal serve-yourself version of the same food; open Mon—Fri between 9 am and 2 pm only, under hair-dresser's salon, no. 113, green door, cognoscenti only, a real find.

LAIGH BAKEHOUSE, 121 Hanover St., bread, gateaux and the richest shortbread in Edinburgh. Open noon—4 pm except Sat. (8 am—12.30 pm).

MOTHER EARTH, St. Stephen St. Recently opened by a group of friendly young people dedicated to producing fine natural foods in a civilised manner—small, cosy, nice sounds. They deserve your palate, open from lunchtime till 11 pm. You may need to book at the weekend.

COUNTRY FARE, Hanover St., Rose St., High St. and FARM-HOUSE, High St., Forrest Rd. For plastic country food.

TOWN & COUNTRY CATERING, William St. close at 5 pm—salads, hot quiches, Bertorelli ices. Delicatessen upstairs will do private catering.

THE DUBLINERS, Dublin St. —coffee house, busy at lunchtime but try it. CHARLOTTE, Rose St., salads, hot dishes. Their reputation rests on their fresh meringues.


## SURVIVAL

The morning after that blow-out meal, if you're absolutely penni-less there are still a few places you can score a meal.

Don't bother these people unless you're in real need—there are plenty of others who are:

Free cups of tea and coffee from the UNIVERSITY CATHOLIC CHAPLAINCY CENTRE, 24 George Sq; LITTLE SISTERS OF THE POOR, 45 Gilmore Pl. will give a meal; PEOPLE IN NEED run a soup kitchen in the Grassmarket, four nights a week in winter, Sunday, Tuesday, Thursday and Saturday, and two nights, Tuesday and Saturday, in summer.

If you are both hungry and have nowhere to stay, the CHURCH OF SCOTLAND SHELTER in Fishmarket Close off the Cowgate will help—mainly used by winos banned from lodging houses.

Rip off a free meal from outside the catering unit, TURNHOUSE AIRPORT, after 11 pm.

Perhaps the nicest free feast is given every Sunday 1—3 pm by HARE KRISHNA, Forrest Rd.

# PUBS

Because of Scotland's archaic licensing laws—now fortunately being reconsidered—you can drink in Edinburgh's five hundred pubs for only eight and a half hours on weekdays: 11.00—14.30 and 17.00—22.00, and only in hotels on Sundays. Ten o'clock is the witching hour in Scotland. But Edinburgh's pubs do offer ways of meeting people, a cheap night out and a wide range of contrasting experiences, from the orgasmic gogo dancing of the King's Wark pub in Leith (pints of beer from 12p) to the cold affluence of the Prestonfield Hotel cocktail bar (peacocks but no draught beer). Edinburgh's pubs can be enjoyed in ones or twos or in a crawl. From the Cafe Royal westwards, Rose St., Edinburgh's Amber Mile, offers nineteen pubs, Leith Walk twenty-six (including five of real quality), and Leith Shore six superbly contrasting boozers. The pubs we can recommend for atmosphere, meeting people, and for cheapness are:

**BENNETS BAR**, Leven St. (nr. Kings Theatre). Actors, workies, and city gents congregate here at lunch and in the evenings for some of Edinburgh's cheapest and best beers. Magnificent nineteenth century interior where mirrors gaze beerily back at you. Ask for Bennets own whiskies.

**FORREST HILL BAR**, Forrest Rd. This is "Sandy Bell's" proclaimed in song, the constantly overflowing haunt of Gaelic speakers, students and folk singers, bringing and playing their violins, accordions, etc. Observe the temperance painting behind the arch halfway down the bar.

**CAFE ROYAL**, West Register St. A famous meeting place for

33

Edinburgh's intellectuals of earlier years, this pub beneath the exclusive restaurant of the same name is sponsored by railwaymen, bus drivers, the financial wizards of St. Andrews Square, but mainly by young people. Reasonably priced beers served in superb Victorian architecture, saved from demolition because of public pressure. If the foorman tries to throw you out, demand to see the manager.

ABBOTSFORD, Rose St. Victorian pub with fine canopied centre bar which has witnessed the beginning of many Rose St. Crawls. Well filled with students and writers every evening. Also good for lunch.

MILNES BAR, Hanover St. Downstairs to join a mixed band of writers, poets, journalists, medics and workers in this politically red pub. Prices cheap, atmosphere pleasant, if sometimes stormy, and easy to reach (and leave) by bus. Less busy in recent years.

JINGLIN' GEORDIE'S, Fleshmarket Close. The best of the city's new pubs and a free house too! 'Scotsman' journalists mix with businessmen and others running for (usually missing) their trains from Waverley. Great unapproachable coal fire in winter. Reasonably cheap.

ST. VINCENT, St. Vincent St. Downstairs to small but remarkably busy and well preserved pub, the centre of freak Edinburgh. Drinks are cheap and the company good.

OLD CHAIN PIER BAR, Leith Shore. Fairly inaccessible but worth the half-hour bus ride from the centre. Study the postcards on the wall and in summer use the verandah to look out on the now pol-

luted Forth.

ENSIGN EWART, Lawnmarket, close to the Castle. Coteries of soldiers and divinity students nightly celebrate the Waterloo hero who died a pauper. Drybrough's beers at acceptable prices.

Other pubs which are worth a visit if you are in the vicinity are the SHEEPS HEID, Duddingston—you can legally drink outside there; RYRIE'S at Haymarket, LESLIE'S on the Causewayside, the COTTARS HOWFF in Rose St., the STAR TAVERN in Northumberland Place, LE CAVEAU DES VINS in Dundas St. (the only wine bar in the city) and SCOTTS—last port of call in Rose Street.

Meeting specific people or groups in pubs is not easy, as rendezvous tend to change as quickly as beer prices. Edinburgh's trendies, fun people and playboys nightly congregate at the JOLLY CARTER and the WORLD in Thistle St., the COTTARS HOWFF and CAFE ROYAL in Rose Street and NICKY TAMS in Victoria St.

Of few political pubs, the WEST END HOTEL, Palmerston Pl. is a Scottish Nationalist stronghold, renowned for the wail of the pibroch and the quaffing of malt whiskies. JENNERS, Princes St., is a last bastion for Tory women, complemented by the NEW TOWN HOTEL, Darnaway St. and many of the plushest hotels. The Liberals retain their own club, 109 Princes St., sadly lacking in members and life but it still serves breakfast at 09.00 and beers until 23.00. The left's sectarianism is reflected in a variety of meeting points round the city—MILNES BAR and the MEADOW, Buccleuch St. recommended. In most working men's pubs the bias is sadly conservative.

You can meet the acting fraternity at the GARRICK, Spittal St. and in BENNETS. The TRAVERSE, Grassmarket, has its own substantial bar, open at lunch and in the evenings from 17.30; it remains open on Sundays. You can meet the press at the DORIC TAVERN, Market St., JINGLIN' GEORDIES, the HALF WAY HOUSE, Fleshmarket Close, the CARLTON HOTEL and the NEW TOWN HOTEL. The press's own club is in Rutland Street.

Student pubs, almost all those around the University, include the WHITE HART INN, Grassmarket, the CAPTAIN'S BAR, College St., the MEADOW, Buccleuch St., CLARK'S BAR, Lady Lawson St., the MORTAR, Forrest Rd. and CHEZ FRED, 34 Castle Terr. There are two spacious bars in the Students University Union, Teviot Row and one in Chambers Street Union, Chambers St.

Pubs also can be experiences in themselves through their wide spectrum of entertainments and it can theoretically at least be the cheapest night out in town. Gogo dancing: fairly recent craze in city pubs, but girls have been doing it for years at the KINGS WARK (a pub restored by Leith Civic Trust!) with its ethnic setting—juke box, cheap ales and drunken sailors. Watch the prices across the road at the MERRYMAKER, with pop group and near striptease designed to delight both sexes. The CANNY MAN, Morningside Rd., has two bars (one topless), but over-expensive drinks.Try also the BRIDGE BAR, Leith Walk, topless, JESS' BAR, West Port, the FOX COVERT, Clermiston Rd. and the RABBIE

BURNS, Gt. Junction St. Gogo dancers appear regularly on Mondays from 5 pm at the old Paddy's Bar, now the TANKARD LOUNGE, Rose St.

## BEER AND SKITTLES

Many pubs have darts, dominoes, and television (usually off in good pubs). Beer mixes expensively with skittles at the ABERCORN INN, Portobello Rd., the HILLBURN ROADHOUSE, the ROBIN'S NEST, Greenend (also gogo girls) and, most attractive of all, the SHEEPS HEID at Duddingston.

## SINGING

Most working men's pubs are good for singsongs especially on paydays, Thursday and Friday. Try especially the HOLYROOD BAR, Holyrood Rd., for ethnic folk singing with a distinctly Irish racial basis. Known locally as the 'Blood Bucket', this is the Edinburgh Irish centre and you can tell from the Celtic photographs that it needs just two lines of the Sash for an unsuspecting fool to start another Boyne. Also, the ARCADE, Cockburn St., the VICTORIA AND ALBERT, Frederick St. (for old music-hall songs) and the GREEN TREE, Gorgie Rd. Spontaneous folk singing guaranteed any night in SANDY BELLS, Forrest Rd. For more info on singing in pubs see Folk and Jazz sections.

You can do the round of the best city pubs—by bus between 17.00 and 22.00 or by hiring a mini-bus from one of the companies named in the Yellow Pages of the telephone directory. Ideal for stag parties and blow-outs.

A full rundown on every one of the city's five hundred pubs is included in the COMPLETE EDINBURGH PUB GUIDE (50p), and an account of the best thirty in the new VISITORS PUB GUIDE.

## STRANGE BREW

People coming to Edinburgh from the deep south are usually stunned by the early closing hours of Scottish pubs. We're told that this was to encourage people to take a "Carry-out" and repair chez lui to continue the revelry and reverie, but what with the rising price of carry-outs it would seem more economic, more potent and more fun to make your own. Beer (and wine) kits are easy to use so long as you follow your particular kit's instructions. It really is very simple.

If you really want to get involved in the home-brew fraternity go along to VIN-BRU at 50 Eastcrosscauseway (Wed. early closing). They have all the gadgetry and literature you will want and they stock all the brands. Otherwise try:

D. NAPIER & SONS, 17 & 18 Bristo Pl. (open 6 days, closed between 1 and 2 pm), or any branch of BOOTS.

Apart from a dustbin (cheapest at Bargain Centre, Lothian St. or Paker Stores, Nicholson Square), you'll need a floating thermometer (Napier's, Bristo Pl. 48p), polythene tubing (Boots, Princes St., 10p per ft., Gray's, George St., 2p per ft!) and your actual bottles.

To bottle, siphon or "rack" the beer through a clear polythene tube or through a siphon-pump (40p Vin-Bru) which can be placed right to the bottom of a 5 gallon dustbin without bringing up sediment.

If you want a fizzy brew put ½ teaspoon of sugar into each bottle before racking the beer; try alternating with ¼ teaspoon of sugar to see which suits your palate.

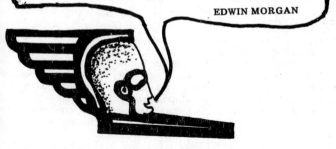

Yes, it is too cold in Scotland for flower people; in any case who would be handed a thistle?

EDWIN MORGAN

# KULTUR

'tiny nippled men'

tiny nippled men wander through the auld toon
in delicate high voices they cry
'we are what you're coming to'

'get away fae me, ye daft poofs'
the big drunk labourer shouts
and falls down the steps into the bog in the grassmarket

## THEATRE

D espite appearances and rumours to the contrary, the
TRAVERSE THEATRE CLUB, 112 West Bow, Grassmarket (226 2633) is not preparing for its centennial celebra-
tions. It still produces some very fine plays at 7:30 and
(frequently) at 10:30 every evening except Monday. Tem-
orary or student membership is cheaper than the real thing,
but it is best to avoid formalities by styling oneself "a
member of Hampstead Theatre Club, which doesn't issue
silly membership cards". The POOL THEATRE CLUB,
76 Hanover St. (225 1850) serves good food and frequently

excellent theatre every weekday lunchtime—performances at 12.15 and 13.15. The club presses on despite major hassles over premises, so watch out for a change of address. The KINGS THEATRE, Tollcross (229 1201) concentrates on conventional touring companies (playing West End oldies), variety, panto, etc. Is also the only decent centre for opera and ballet in the East. The LYCEUM, Grindlay St. (229 4353) stages a usually good rep season. Students get in cheap (except Saturdays) via matriculation card. The CHURCH HILL THEATRE, Mornigside Rd. (447 7596): mainly amateur productions, those reasonably well advertised are usually worth considering.

30 miles out of Edinburgh in Milnathort, Kinross-shire, there is LEDLANET NIGHTS (Kinross 2224 or 2391) which rewards the audience with a rather more varied bill. BRUNTON THEATRE, Musselburgh (665 2240) seems to have lost its theatrical pedigree somewhere, but nevertheless its modern dance productions are good.

The Festival isn't what it's cracked up to be, theatrically. Good but boring productions of oldies hold the floor. The Fringe isn't a lot better—best guides to Festival time are to be found in 'Cracker' and the 'Scotsman'.

Formal theatrical education in Edinburgh is too reactionary to be worth mentioning. If you want to do your thing on or around the streets of Edinburgh, there are several possible contacts:
THEATRE WORKSHOP, 66 Hanover St. (226 6808)—moving soon.

39

APES, Active People's Entertainment Service, c/o Anne Flint, 20 Waverley Pk. Theatre—especially dance drama.

ARTS PROJECTS (EDINBURGH), 9 Straiton Pl., Portobello, Edin. 15 (669 1449)—a group of people working at grass roots level, closely connected with an exciting proposed multi media centre in Leith.

EDINBURGH UNIVERSITY DRAMATIC SOCIETY, Societies Centre, Hill Place.

## CINEMAS

The nearest Edinburgh has to Alternative Cinema is the Edinburgh International Film Festival (late August). For the rest of the time the normal fare is general release films and re-runs. To find out what's on read 'Cracker', 'Student' or the 'Evening News'. Best crits in the 'Scotsman'. Meanwhile here's a short and snappy rundown on existing cinemas

The NATIONAL FRILM THEATRE (Film House), 3 Randolph Cres. (225 1671) has at last decided to turn itself into a part repertory, part trendy-foreign film art house. In the same building as the NFT is the EDINBURGH FILM GUILD (225 1671). Membership fee £3, films

free to members. Members can buy in advance undated guest tickets (25p).

EDINBURGH UNIVERSITY FILM SOCIETY (£2 for students, £3 for public), three times a week, Sun., Wed. and Fri., in the Odeon, George Sq. Theatre or Appleton Tower. Members can buy undated guest tickets, at 25p, for certain performances. The only other club of sorts in town is at the FRENCH INSTITUTE, 13 Randolph Cres. (225 5366). All films free to members. Temporary membership one week 25p. Occasionally throws up a rare surprise.

For the general release films and re-runs Edinburgh is particularly well-endowed. The ABC FILM CENTRE, Lothian Rd. (229 3030) has three cinemas. It was intended that the smallest cinema should be given over to art films but the dictates of moneymaking has almost put a stop to that, though occasional ones still slip through. The other two cinemas in the complex are given over to road shows and occasional big films like 'The Godfather', 'Lady Sings the Blues', 'Clockwork Orange', etc. The ODEON, S. Clerk St. (667 3513), a Rank cinema, provides a home for the Bond movies and such as 'Cabaret', but being one large auditorium has a rather slow turnover of films. To compensate it runs a dynamic series of late night shows, with everything from the complete Russian 'War and Peace' to 15 episodes of 'Flash Gordon'. The CAMEO, Tollcross (229 6822) occasionally comes up with a first release though tends to bring back safe second run winners like 'Decameron'. The PLAYHOUSE, Greenside Pl., Leith Walk (556 7266), because of its massive auditorium, tends to go in for value for money double bills, e.g. 'Butch Cassidy'/'Mash'. The DOMINION, Churchill (447 2660) —newly renovated twin cinema providing similar fare. The JACEY, Princes St., which closed during the past year will be sadly missed by the gaberdine cowboy brigade.The CALEY,Lothian Rd.(229 7670) goes in for family epics, but runs a summer season of late night films mainly pop extravaganzas, e.g. 'Gimme Shelter', The TIVOLI, Gorgie Rd., Tynecastle (337 1911), ASTORIA, Corstorphine (334 3002), RITZ, Rodney St. (556 4325), LA SCALA, Nicolson St. (667 1839) and GEORGE, Bath St., Portobello (669 2779) tend to go in for anything that makes money. The SALON, Baxters Pl. (556 7395) changes its programme every three days and is very cheap. Smells of disinfectant, but is a glorious place to catch up on old classics.

If you want to organise your own film shows, the POLITKINO CLUB, 11 Greek St., London (film distributors) may help.

## ART GALLERIES
There are six 'standard' art galleries in Edinburgh; of these one charges admission and the rest are free, though this is liable to change in the near future. For further info on these galleries see any straight tourist guide.

ROYAL SCOTTISH ACADEMY, Princes St. Open weekdays 10.00—17.00, Sun. 14.00—17.00. Adults 15p, children 5p. NATIONAL GALLERY OF SCOTLAND, the Mound. Open weekdays 10.00—17.00, Sun. 14.00—17.00. Free. SCOTTISH NATIONAL PORTRAIT GALLERY, Queen St. Open weekdays 10.00—17.00, Sun. 14.00—17.00. Free. SCOTTISH NATIONAL GALLERY OF MODERN ART, Botanical Gdns. Open weekdays 10.00—18.00, Sun. 14.00—17.00. Free. SCOTTISH ARTS COUNCIL GALLERY, 19 Charlotte Sq. Open weekdays 10.00—18.00, Sun. 14.00—17.00. Free. CITY OF EDINBURGH ART CENTRE, Calton Hill.

Edinburgh also has numerous smaller commercial galleries which frequently present interesting exhibitions.

RICHARD DEMARCO GALLERY, 8 Melville Cres. Open weekdays 10.30—17.30, Sat. 10.00—14.00. The ENGLISH SPEAKING UNION GALLERY, 22 Atholl Cres. IAN CLARKSON GALLERY, 87 West Bow. GREAT KING ST. GALLERY, 12 Gt. King St. Open weekdays 10.00—18.00, Sat. 10.00—13.00. The TORRANCE GALLERY, 296 Dundas St. Open weekdays 11.00—18.00, Sat. 10.30—13.00. DOUGLAS AND FOULIS, 9 Castle St. AITKEN DOTT, THE SCOTTISH GALLERY, 26 Castle St. KES MOSAICS, 33 Alva St. TALBOT RICE ART CENTRE, Old College, South

Bridge. SCOTTISH CRAFT CENTRE, Acheson House, Canongate. LETHAM GALLERY, 45 Cumberland St. DANIEL SHACKLETON GALLERY, 74 Thistle St. JOHN MATHIESON & SON, 20 Frederick St. NEW 57 GALLERY, 105 Rose St. ALL ART DISPLAY LTD., 16a Ainslie Pl. Free, open Mon—Sat, 10.00—17.30.

# WORKSHOPS

There are in addition numerous workshops with good facilities in Edinburgh.

PRINTMAKERS WORKSHOP, 46 Victoria St. Equipment for lithography, screenprinting and etching. Most necessary materials are included in the fees. Tuition 20p per hour. Membership costs £1 p.a. Open Tues—Sat. 10.00—18.00 and Thurs. 18.00—21.00. SILKSCREEN WORKSHOP, 76 Hanover St. Has printing frames and photo-stencil equipment. Fees approx. £5 a month, not including materials, tuition available. WEAVERS WORKSHOP, Monteith House, Royal Mile. Weaving studios, dyeing facilities, implements, space for exhibitions and lectures. Tuition is given in four graded ten-week gourses. Fees for tuition £5.50 per course. Open all week 09.30—10.30. CERAMIC WORKSHOP, 15/16 Victoria Terr. Facilities for artists and potters. Materials are also on sale. Fees £1 per day or £3.50 per week, membership costs £2.50 p.a. Open weekdays 09.00—17.00, Sat. 09.00—14.00. EDINBURGH SCHOOL OF ART, Lauriston Pl. runs a wide range of night classes in design, painting and drawing. Fees for two terms one evening per week £4.50.

# MUSEUMS

Those that are free are mentioned, though probably all will charge by summer '74.

ROYAL SCOTTISH MUSEUM, Chambers St. Open weekdays 10.00—17.00, Sun. 14.00—17.00. Free. The largest comprehensive museum of science and art in the UK. Good reasonably cheap cafeteria. NATIONAL MUSEUM OF ANTIQUITIES, Queen St. Open weekdays 10.00—17.00 (Festival 10.00—20.00), Sun 14.00—17.00. Free. Relics of everyday life in Scotland from the Stone Age. LADY STAIR'S HOUSE, Lawnmarket. Open Mon—Fri 10.00—16.00, Sat 10.00—13.00. Adults 5p, children 2½p. A museum commemorating Burns, Scott and Stevenson. HUNTLY HOUSE, Canongate. Open weekdays 10.00—17.00. Adults 5p, children 2½p. The building dates from 1591, and was at one time the Council House and Prison of the Canongate. It now contains a collection of Highland Dress and Tartans, also a collection of water colours of Old Edinburgh. MUSEUM OF CHILDHOOD, 34 High St. Open Mon—Sat 10.00—17.00. Adults 5p, children 2½p. The CASTLE, open Mon—Sat 09.30—18.00, Sun 11.00—18.00. Precincts only, open until 21.00. Admission to Historical Apt., adults 15p, children 5p. PALACE OF HOLYROOD HOUSE, foot of Canongate. Open (mid-June to mid-Sept.) weekdays 09.30—18.00, Sun 11.00—18.00; winter and spring weekdays 09.30—16.30, Sun 12.30—16.30. Adults 15p, children 5p. TRANSPORT MUSEUM, Shrubhill Leith Walk. Open weekdays 10.00—19.00. Free. The museum illustrates the historical development of transport in Edinburgh. ST. CECILIA'S HALL, Cowgate. Open Sat only 14.00—17.00. 15p entrance, children must be accompanied. A fine exhibition of old musical instruments.

For those interested, there are other museums, houses and sites of historical interest open to the public. For information about these, ask at the Edinburgh Tourist Office for the pamphlet on Museums in Edinburgh.

# MUSIC

## ROCK

Edinburgh has never come up with a rock band;nobody has really made it since the Incredible String Band (with Clive Palmer) or Bert Jansch.Generally Edinburgh music doesn't have the guts or balls of Glasgow music, and bands who try and make that have not worked out. Edinburgh's cultural approach is more subtle, more inclined to 'head' music, like jazz (Nexus) or folksy Folk. Mama Flyer, perhaps the best rock band on the Edinburgh scene, seem to have the subtleties as well as the appeal.

1973 is the first year of the Edinburgh Pop Festival, promoted by Bruce Finlay, and co-ordinated by Pete Irvine (ex-Rock Factory). Held at the Empire Theatre—should be interesting, and next year hopes to be even bigger and better. Major tours usually include the Empire, Nicholson St. (2000 seats), where the bouncers are world famous (for heaviness), and the acoustics mediocre. Smaller tours tend to be handled by the Odeon, South Clerk St., and the Caley, Lothian Rd., although they have had heavy bands in the past (Wishbone Ash, Hawkwind, Uriah Heep). The Odeon also indulges in Saturday morning gigs for kids but check by phone first. Unicorn Leisure (Glasgow agents 041332 5096) have taken over the New Cavendish in Tollcross and renamed it Clouds. Chris McClure and Salvation are fairly regular guests in the lower room, but the disco upstairs seems to absorb most of their imagination and effort. The University has been responsible for bringing some much needed talent to Edinburgh, but gigs are only put on during the term time. The University Refectory in Bristo St. is the scene of most of the gigs but the McEwan Hall across the road has also been used on occasion. The Traverse in the Grassmarket sometimes has late concerts, mainly Mama Flyer. Cat Iron, in Cephas Cellar, Stafford St., is Edinburgh's only regular rock club for listening audiences. The intention is to be as non-commercial as possible, helping to promote small but good bands—nice idea. There is very little in the way of free concerts in Edinburgh—although Leith Festival have a concert on the Links which includes the best of the local bands each year.

Some of the better bands knocking around Edinburgh at the moment are:

MAMA FLYER, definitely the band most likely to... They are going to be very busy but jam with friends under the name of Footprints. Phone Pete, 556 9615.

ST. CLEMENTS WELL, folk-rock group recently signed to Bell, phone Alan Shepherd, 225 2424.

IRON VIRGIN, Edinburgh's top pop band playing lots of town hall bops.

SILLY WIZARD, BEN GUN, VALHALLA, EAST WEST, and SCHARNHORST are all worth watching out for.

## ORGANISING GIGS

Calls for a lot more skill than you might suppose to avoid crashing to earth in a welter of bills. The top groups are all so expensive that combined with the cost of a hall it would be better to work through an established promoters. A better bet if you really want to get your own thing together is search out for promising groups while they're still cheap, and get a signed contract some months in advance. If your judgement's good you may find you've got a first class concert for little more than the cost of the hall.

A nice guy with a lot of music experience is Pete Irvine (556 9615).

## AGENCIES

You may well have to go through London to get the groups you really want; COMMUNITY MUSIC run by Ian King, c/o BIT, London (01-229 8219) could give you a lot of help in organising bookings. The nearest agencies to Edinburgh are in Glasgow, AME (041-556 1241) and UNICORN LEISURE (041-332 5096). For recording studios try RADIO EDINBURGH (229 9657), who not only have the equipment but are also good people. ASSOCIATED ENTERTAINMENTS Recording Studio, 68 Craighall Rd. (552 2671) is OK but more expensive.

## DISCOS

O ur resident swinger wouldn't really recommend any of the

discos in Edinburgh, but if you just want to dance your blues away, put on your high-heeled sneakers and you'll be accommodated in one of the following:

WALKERS, Shandwick Pl. Open Mon—Sat. 18.30—23.00. Must buy a meal, 15p, or leave at 20.00. Over 18's. Decor aspires to the elegance of a Parisian salon but the purple lights and the wooden plank floor betray that illusion. The clientele is made up of groovers manque, who gyrate bedroom-mirror-rehearsed movements. OK for a pick-up, comfortable and the music, like all the city's discos, has a very commercial, black funk flavour. FLANNIGANS, Rose St. North Lane. Open Sun—Thurs. 21.30—02.00, Fri & Sat 21.30—03.00. Over 21's. Is jam packed, hot and humid. The kids there dance like dervishes, the collective cool being maintained by 'dickie'-clad heavies. VALENTINO'S/MUSCULAR ARMS, East Fountainbridge. Open Fri 19.30—01.00, Sat 19.30—24.00. It's the kind of place you dangle car keys even if you've never owned one. The dress is 'liberal-smartish', but doormen are claimed to be discriminating. The place is so roomy that you can take a girl and have shaded intimacy, or go in a group and take over. No licence, but two pubs attached. Best looking, best music, best value, but better to go in couples. The AMERICANA, Fountainbridge. Open Mon—Sun. 21.30—02.30. Over 20's. Is Edinburgh's little Chicago, converted from a meat market to a cattle market in the Tollcross stockmarket. They're all there, Dutsch Schaltz, Big Al, flunks and floozies, heavies that are overbearingly heavy, bouncers that vehemently bounce and teeny boppers that infrequently bop. Most certainly untouchable. VARSITY DISCO, Nicolson St. Open Fri and Sat, 21.00—02.00. Over 21's. Claims to be in the business purely for LSD (not the -diethylamide variety). NEW INTERNATIONAL CLUB, Princes St. Open every weeknight till 01.30, 02.30 weekends. AQUARIUS, Grindlay St. Open 17.00—23.00, 7 nights. Licence till 22.00, supper licence 22.00—23.00. Over 21's.

## JAZZ

It is unfortunate that, apart from appearances by the Jacques Loussier trio during the Festival and occasional forays north by bands like Chris Barber, jazz in Edinburgh seems to be entirely restricted to a basic Dixie style, embellished here and there by a dash of soul and rhythm and blues. There are currently about three or four bands playing in Edinburgh, to some extent their personnel are interchangeable. The typical line-up is the well-tried six-piece ensemble: three rhythm and three up front.

Despite criticisms it might be that we should be thankful for what we've got. Regular weekly appearances are made by NEXUS, a good six-piece ensemble who are reviving mainstream bop at the Royal Mile Centre (alternate Mondays)

47

and Nicky Tams (Wednesdays). CHARLIE MacNAIRS seven-piece group is playing traditional jazz at the Yellow Carvel, the Tron (Thursday & Friday), and the White Cockade (Wednesday). His raps are worth listening to as much as the music. KENNY RAMAGE, HEADS (based in the east of Scotland but occasionally visiting Edinburgh) and FOOTPRINTS (elements of Mama Flyer put together by ex-Mama Flyer trumpeter John McNicol) are all worth seeing when they are performing here. The Cephas Club in Shandwick Place has jazz at various times over the weekend, but check the timing first. More information on what's going on from the Secretary of the Jazz Appreciation Society, c/o University Union, Teviot Row (667 2091).

## FOLK MUSIC

Folk music is essentially ephemeral and amorphous, so check the details of places and times that we give as they are liable to change.

### PUBS AND HOTELS

NB closing time 22.00. GROSVENOR HOTEL, Grosvenor St. Sunday evenings. Pay to get in, easier to hear than see, popular with performers, Irish/Scottish/singalong sort of things. WAVERLEY BAR, St. Mary's St. Small, warm, crowded, different groups six nights a week. Atmosphere good, sometimes so good it drowns out singers. NICKY TAMS, Victoria St. Here they hire a group to do every night for a week. No floor singers, standards, C & W, etc. SANDY BELLS, Forrest Rd. Spontaneous folk music as the city's Gaels mix with students in the University area's smallest and most exciting pub.

Drunken rumours have been heard of distant folksinging in other places: YELLOW CARVEL, Hunter's Sq., Mon, Tues, Wed. KELLY'S CAVERN, Royal Terr., Sun. The WHITE COCKADE and TANKARD LOUNGE, both Rose St. The ROYAL ARCHER, Jeffrey St., Tues and Thurs.

### CLUBS

Usually an entry charge, often membership rules, which are sometimes flexible, so ask/borrow card/get signed in/smile sweetly; mainly dry, if you take your own refreshment be tactful and prepared to give way. Monday, the BUFFS, 12 Albany St. Membership/signing in/smile. Some good traditional guests, fair residents, some floor singing, large hot audiences. Tuesday, CATHOLIC STUDENTS UNION, George Sq. Term Time only, alternate Tuesdays. New, small, but attentive audience and relaxed atmosphere—good. Wednesday, the COFFIN CLUB, Cephas Cellar, off Stafford St. Late night, very large and noisy, just-out-of-the-pub audience, with a love for the 'Wild Rover' again and again.

Friday, the CROWN, otherwise Edinburgh University Folksoc, Hill Pl. Wide range of music and standards. Join/show membership card/smile. Saturday, the TRIANGLE, 7 Randolph Pl. In the YWCA, young, quiet audience, some good singing—try it. Sunday, no joy, no clubs, no pubs, no carry-outs. Just hotels—Grosvenor, Kelly's Cavern, Park Hotel, etc.

# CLASSICAL

For those who would complain that when the Festival comes to an end the city becomes once more a cultural backwater, here is a drop of concentrated classical goodness.

SCOTTISH NATIONAL ORCHESTRA plays Fridays October to April, often with international soloists and under guest conductors, in the drab, acoustically indifferent Usher Hall, Lothian Rd. No price concessions but Upper Tier seats are not outrageously expensive, and give the best sound picture anyway, despite usually sweltering atmosphere. By joining the SNO Friends (students 75p, under 18 50p, contact SNO, 150 Hope St., Glasgow, 041-332 7244) you can sit in on rehearsals. Ticket agency—Edinburgh Bookshop, George St. SCOTTISH OPERA: their season is in May/June at the Kings; at E.I.F. (Aug/Sept.) and occasionally for short seasons at other times of the year in the Lyceum. Student concessions (tickets for unsold seats at 50p, 5 mins. before performance time). CHORAL RECITALS are usually given (free) at 18.00 before the 18.30 service in St. Giles Cathedral, High St. ORGAN RECITALS are often given free in the University—see the University Bulletin. For other professional and amateur concerts see 'Music in Edinburgh' (25p) for dates, times and venues, and the local press. Booking agents Rae Macintosh and Edinburgh Bookshop, both George St. Students (i.e. young people) often receive price concessions, if they have identification—so take, or fake, a Student ID Card. REID CONCERTS—University Music Faculty, Park Pl. Generally on Thursdays, but check. Under composer/Professor Kenneth Leighton, pursuing adventurous programme policy. Orchestral concerts by Reid Orchestra, choral, chamber music, and recitals. Free—you are encouraged to buy a moderately priced programme. University also holds concerts in St. Cecilia's Hall, Cowgate. See pamphlet 'Music in the University' from Music Faculty, University, phone 667 1011, ext. 2584.

Music making: Outlets for amateur musicians seeking an opportunity to play or sing together range from the Occasional Orchestra through the Savoy Opera Group and the Festival Chorus to ad hoc chamber music ensembles. The Musicians Union offers its members the opportunity to perform (details from the secretary). University music includes several orchestras (auditions are the rule), the University singers, the Glee Club, the University Choir (no auditions). Contact Secretary of the Music Faculty (667 1011 ext. 2572). Announcements of new musical ventures and requests for personnel may appear occasionally in the local press.

# LATE NIGHT.

The capital has a good night life if you know where to look for it! So, get out and do it.

**Theatre**

The Traverse Theatre, West Bow (bar and restaurant till 23.00—box office 226 2633) and the Pool Theatre, Hanover St. hold late night performances of plays, rock music and jazz. Sometimes! Check these out with current edition of Cracker, or phone direct. Become a member and get some outersight benefits. The Pool is closing temporarily, but watch out for new premises.

**Cinema**

Only a handful of cinemas in Edinburgh show late night films, and program schedules are quite erratic.

CALEY, Lothian Rd, each evening throughout the summer at 22.45.
ODEON, South Clerk St. usually Fridays and Saturdays at 23.15.

CAMEO, Tollcross, usually Fridays at 23.15.
EDINBURGH FILM FESTIVAL, Randolph Cresc. every night throughout Festival at 22.45.

Check out these possibilities with the latest edition of the Evening News, (Entertainments section), or get a current copy of Cracker for full information on the arts.

## Discotheques

If you've got stamina, but no imagination treck on over to the Americana, Fountainbridge till 2.00, Flannigan's Rose Street till 2.00 (3.00 Fri/Sat.)

Valentinos, beside Muscular Arms, Fountainbridge, can be recommended (good decor and atmosphere).

## Restaurants

This city can boast of some really good restaurants which open till early morning. If you feel hungry after theatre or cinema, get on over to these which are open beyond midnight.

THE PALUMBO, 40-41 Bruntsfield Place (229 5025) nightly till 1.00. Good Italian menu; stuffed peppers with seafood a speciality. Can cost you over £1.

BELLA NAPOLI, 32-34 Grindlay Street (229 5757) Midnight (Mon/Thurs). 1.00 (Fri/Sat). Italian cuisine. Pizza Neapolitan baked in special wood oven!

LOON FUNG, Howard Place (Inverleith Row) (556 1781) 2.00 including Sundays. Best Chinese in town! Look out for Lemon Chicken!

WELL MET, Gilmour Place. Open till 2.00. No. 2 Chinese in town.

WOODVILLE, 9-11 Barclay Place (near King's Theatre). (229 1781). Open to 1.00 seven nights—Cheap.

THE SORRENTO, 15 Albert Place, (554 7282) 0.30 Mon-Thurs; 1.00 Fri-Sat; midnight Sunday. Italian food and wines—try escalop of veal.

SANS SOURRI Restaurant, Royal Chimes Club, Royal Terrace. Till 3.00, no license but open to non-members.

CASA SICILIANA, 11 Lochrin Terrace (229 1690). Only Sicilian in town. Open till 1.00 — £1.50.

Almost all good restaurants in the city stay open till 23.00, (some with extensions for the Festival e.g. Eighty Queen Street). So move into these places just before then, and order big!.

**Tarry's Hot Food Delivery Service** (334 1893) will deliver food to your home up to 23.00, minimum order 50p. Otherwise, the Cornerstone Cafe, St. John's Vaults, Lothian Rd. is a late night coffee house, open till midnight on Friday, 1.00 on Saturday and 11.30 on Sunday. Run by West End Churches, it serves reasonably priced snacks and offers music and discussion—a useful meeting place.

Also open till 1.00 nightly are the medium priced Conal Eating House, 100 Lothian Rd. and La Roma, 29 Clerk St.

If you're plain and simply hungry and want a cheap meal to satify your appetite, a range of fish and chip shops remain open till midnight. Note the following if you're in their proximity.

THE METROPOLE, Torphichen St. Edinburgh's latest opening cafe, medium priced meals till 4.00.

THE GOLDEN ARROW, 133 Lauriston Pl. 2.00 nightly (4.00 Fri/Sat). Pies and chips from 14p. Not attractive.

SERGIO'S, 131 Lauriston Pl. 2.00 weekdays, 4.00 Fri/Sat. Usual selection of chip shop foods.

WEST NICHOLSON FISH RESTAURANT, 35 West Nicholson St. 1.00 nightly (4.00 Fri/Sat). Reasonable.

ERASMOS, 3 Sciennes, (nr. Meadows) Fish and Chips to 1.00.

THE MERMAID, 45 Leith Walk. Fish and chips to 1.00.

DEEP SEA II, 10 Union Pl. 2.00 (Fri/Sat), otherwise midnight. More inviting than Deep Sea I.

MARTY'S GRILL, West Maitland St. 23.30 weekdays, 16.00 Fri/Sat. snacks.

## Drinks

Bars and pubs in Edinburgh close at 22.00 and that's that! If you want to drink after 10 pm make for a licenced restaurant, order a meal, and extend your drinking up time by an hour. These places can be packed out at weekends so move in early.

To guard against a potentially "dry" evening buy a traditional carry-out (a bag full of assorted booze), before 10pm from any pub, but it's cheaper to purchase your carry-out from an off-sales so look around.

AUGUSTUS BARNETT, Hillhouse Rd. (332 8440)—cheapest in town.

ODDBINS, Inverleith Row.

HENDERSONS, Tollcross.

Become the guest of a hotel resident; obtain a late license for a function.

## Parties

The real night life is the student party scene. Make contact through the grapevine of student activities. Socialise and make friends with students at any of these rendezvous.

DAVID HUME TOWER (DHT), basement cafeteria, George Square.

UNIVERSITY LIBRARY basement coffee room.

STUDENTS' HEALTH CENTRE, Bristo Street, cafeteria.
MEADOW BAR, Buccleuch Street.
ST. VINCENT BAR—top of St. Steven's Street.
BENNETS BAR, next door to King's Theatre.
THE ART COLLEGE, Lauriston Place.

Better still, organise your own party; use your pad; or a friend's, hire out a pub's facilities. First get your hip friends together and take it from there.

Take advantage of warm evenings to get an out-of-doors barbecue together. Edinburgh has some really nice environs. Pick a green area on the map and head out there. Best places are Cramond Beach. Good silvery sands; head up river. Real cool! Try Silverknowes Parkland, between Granton and Cramond. Calton hill etc. Don't let rain spoil your night—just get closer together!

For your own flat party you need:- sounds, space and booze; and mountains of food! that's essential. Breweries will sell you drink directly at cheaper than normal prices if you can guarantee a regular order—or at least say you will. Contact the sales dept. of the major breweries listed in Yellow Pages. Cheap booze can also be obtained from any of the following good Off Licences in the city.

FAIRBAIRNS, 11 Albert St. 2 days' notice. Barrels, 88 pints, from £7.80.
SHERS, Fowler Terrace.
KAYYAMS, junction of Albert St.—Easter Rd.

You can hire mobile discotheques from any one of almost seventy groups in the city. Costs are variable depending on distance and playing time—but expect to pay up to £10 for a top disco. Your best bet is to phone for an estimate giving a few days' notice. You can also hire go-go dancers, given more notice. The best though not the cheapest we know, are:

| Spinning Wheel | 667 2914 |
| Noise Invasion | 667 4968 |
| One Step Beyond | 667 2097 |
| Revolva | 337 1048 |

## Take over a Pub

If you can't get a flat party together, then take over a hotel or a pub with a late licence, or hire a hall. A late licence can be obtained for a special function held on licensed premises e.g. 21sts, stag parties (Yuch!), engagements, etc. Dig? Approach manager of premises and ask him to apply for extension of licensing hours for your function and sign the appropriate forms. Let magistrates and Chief Constable take care of the rest. Give plenty of notice.

Events

If you want to organise your event in the shape of a concert, get in touch with Corporation (for hiring halls) and see FUN section.

## Late Night Food Shops

For late night milk, try Murchies, Lochrin Buildings (opp. King's Theatre) or St. Cuthberts, Morrison Street. Rattle gates and shout!

If you happen to run out of food to prepare, don't despair. Here's a list of late night general stores that can help you through:

PHILLIPS, 48 Blackfriars St. Cowgate. 1.30 and beyond. Latest in town.

GENERAL AND ORIENTAL GROCERS, 49 London St. Midnight Good veg/fruit.

GERRY's, 21 Grassmarket, 23.00 (exc. Saturdays).

NICK'S, Canongate. 23.00. Ice Cream a speciality.

SUNRISE GENERAL GROCERS, 94 Dalry Rd. 23.00 (open 8.00.) Cut price groceries.

QUERNSTONE, Lochrin Buildings (opp. Kings). Ice cream/sweets. 23.00.

TOBACCONISTS, 234 Dalry Rd. 23.00. Milk. Tobacco.

CORNER STORES, Caledonian—Dalry Rd. junction. Cheap groceries 22.00.

THE LARDER, Raeburn St.—Dean St. junction. 22.00. Expensive.

Bakeries

Hey, do you realise that no one need go hungry at nights in this capital! For appeasing late, late night starvation, make for the nearest bakery. Most open between 22.00-24.00 (except Saturdays), and will serve you freshly made rolls, scones, doughnuts and pastries, if you use the back door. Be friendly, they're performing an act of revolutionary love!

From long experience, we can recommend the following, with opening times.

ANDERSON'S, 5 St. Patrick Sq. 23.00

DOUGLAS, 7 Bakers Pl. Stockbridge. 22.00.

OVENFRESH BAKERY, Morrison St. Midnight to 2.00.

LAWRENCES BAKERY, 5 Yeoman Pl. Midnight. Shop open on Fridays.

CRAIG-GREEN BAKERY, 8 St. Peters Building. 1.00.

REDBRAES BAKERY, 137a Broughton St. Midnight.

## Travelling

Moving late at night is expensive and can be a hassle! Minimum taxi fare is 21p (best services are 229 6336, and 229 5221—see Yellow Pages), but if you want to save money, get to know inside out how the late night bus service from 00.15 to 4.15 operates (pick up a night bus service timetable from Transport Information Centre on Waverley Bridge).

The night bus service operates from Monday night to Friday night inclusive, and the complete circular route fare costs 12p. Gauge where it's going to pick you up by remembering that all buses pass the east end of Princes Street (Waverley area) at 15 mins before and after the hour. Don't miss it!

The bus routes are:—

Service No. 1. Lochend-Corstorphine circular Restalrig Rd, Leith Wlk, Princes St, Haymarket, Stevenson Dr, Broomhouse, Corstorphine Rd, Haymarket and back.

Service No. 2. Portobello-Comiston circular Portobello High St. London Rd, Princes St, Lothian Rd, Tollcross, Colinton Rd, Oxgangs, Morningside Rd, Tollcross and back.

Service No. 3 Leith-Clermiston circular Leith Wlk, Ferry Rd, Leith Wlk, Princes St, Haymarket, Corstorphine Rd, Drum Brae, Davidsons Mains, Haymarket and back.

Service No. 4. Craigmillar-Muirhouse circular Hay Dr, Prestonfield, Clerk St, Princes St, Frederick St, Comely Bank, Muirhouse and back.

Service No. 5. Hyvots Bank-Granton Rd. circular Hyvots Bank, Kaimes, Minto St, Waverley, Inverleith, Golden Acre, Granton Rd. and back.

If you're on wheels and need help your best bet is the AA (225 8464) or RAC 229 3555) even if you're not a member. Don't be conned into paying above normal rates—

rather wait till the morning. Twenty-four hour garages for petrol and other accessories are—

ALEXANDER'S, Fountainbridge. (Self-service, one delivery pump only English £1 notes).

H & G S Bell Ltd, 4 Brunswick St. (off London Rd.
JONES MOTOR HOUSE, Falcon Ave.

LINKS GARAGE LTD, Bruntsfield Pl. (Self-service only, one delivery pump takes coins).

MEADOWBANK AUTO POINT, 63 London Rd.

WINDMILL SERVICE STATION (Esso), Craigleith, Queensferry Rd.

ROSS MOTORS (Edinburgh) Ltd. 4 Ratcliffe Terr. (also car wash and wax).

M.J. SLOAN & Co. Ltd., Belford Road.

SMT SALES AND SERVICES Co. Ltd. Haymarket Terr. (petrol and car hire).

MOIR & BAXTER LTD, Comely Bank.

BURMAH, Meadowbank (Discount and stamps).

## Night Services

For minor ailments, headaches, toothaches, etc, try fish and chip shops. Most carry a range of vital necessities. For medical help, head for Boots the Chemist, Shandwick Place (West End). They're the last chemists to close, at 22.00 (Sundays at 18.00).

For serious ailments, make rapidly for the Outpatients. emergency services of any hospital, particularly the Royal Infirmary, Lauriston Place (229 2477).

## Tomorrow's Papers

Scotsman, Daily Record and Express can be purchased every night from 23.00 at Tollcross, Shandwick Place; and Princes Street.


HAVE A GOOD TIME—WE ARE!

It's hard enough for people who actually live in Edinburgh to get decent cheap accommodation but for the visitor on a limited budget there are extra difficulties. The number of tourists mounts up each year and exploitation increases as the building of large hotels goes on. This section deals mainly with the best ways to avoid that exploitation.

For general information on accommodation the Tourist Information and Accommodation Service, 1 Cockburn St. (226 6591) will help. They're open 0900-2100 (Sunday 1100-2100) during the summer season and 0900-1800 during the winter (Saturday 0900-1300, closed Sunday). They also run a night-answering service for tourists. Student residences can also be booked outside term-time through the Student Accommodation and Welfare Service, 7 Buccleuch Place. Best publications to look at are the **Edinburgh Tourist Accommodation Register** (available free

57

from 1 Cockburn St.), and the **Scottish Youth Hostels Handbook**. Also see the **Scotsman** and the **Evening News** each day. Notice boards at any student centre, union or newsagents advertise cheapest places to stay temporarily.

## Sleeping Free

Sleeping by starlight is difficult—and often wet—in Edinburgh. The law declares sleeping in parks illegal, but the police are hardly likely to enforce this by arrest. They will, however, treat you very suspiciously, probably take your name and generally keep you from a decent sleep by asking repeatedly that you move on. It's best to find a place where you can't possibly disturb or offend anyone and pick up any litter when you go. Remember the more remote you are, the safer you are from disturbance. Sleeping in Princes St. Gdns., George Sq., Calton Hill or Blackford Park means climbing over the fence after closing time and a strong possibility of being disturbed. Places that can't be locked up are the Meadows (rather public and most of its benches are populated by winos and down-and-outs) and Holyrood Park (exposed to the elements). If you're really down and don't mind dingy surroundings or wine fumes, try the all-night shelter at Fishmarket Close in the Cowgate (places for 40 to 50 people).

Waverley Station waiting room is open all night but station security is fairly strict: purchase a ticket from Waverley to Haymarket (6p) and you are technically allowed to wait there, or find out when a conveniently timed long distance train is due and say you're waiting to meet someone off it. The bus station in St. Andrew Square also has a few shelters which can't be locked, but you can forget about Turnhouse Airport—it's too far away and its waiting lounge is too small.

Other ways of sleeping free are on the beach or in a car or van. Cramond beach is beautiful when morning comes—there is also an unattended car park there if you want to sleep in your vehicle. Generally for sleeping in your car or van anywhere in Edinburgh it's as well to drive out of the city centre—otherwise the police will ask questions. It's a waste of time trying handles of parked cars—even if you're successful Big Brother is hardly likely to believe you only wanted to sleep there. Finally, if you're really stuck ask at a police station for use of an empty cell.

## Crashpads

If you're short of the ready and the rain's falling the best thing to do is crash someone's flat. The people most likely to give you a place on their floor are students—ask around the various student refectories and unions in Edinburgh. There are certain unwritten rules for anyone crashing—1) be sociable 2) don't scrounge 3) help clean up the flat. Remember that your attitudes and behaviour in the flat can encourage the occupants to take others later. Help had a list of people willing to give space, free, to temporary visitors. So much money and property were stolen the list dwindled to nothing. Nevertheless Help does hope to build up some more eventually so you could try them at 554 6908. Edinburgh University SRC also offers emergency accommodation at 47 Forrest Road—depending on demand, they might take temporary visitors. They charge 25p per night there for the first seven nights, rising by about 7½p per night for the second week (pay weekly in advance). The normal maximum period of residence is 14 nights. You must book through the SRC office, Chambers Street, (667 1290).

## Hostels

Not surprisingly, these are usually cheaper than small hotels. There are several in Edinburgh but their functions and prices, and the requirements for your eligibility, vary. In most you can expect showers, baths, communal lounge and TV room, and where there are separate rooms look for a washhand basin, wardrobe and heating. Most also issue late keys.

POLLOCK HALLS, 69 Dalkeith Rd. (667 4331). Accepts students and non-students, late June to late September. Eight separate 'halls', each providing single room accommodation. A good deal for students—£1.08 a night bed & breakfast (no full board for students). Non-students pay £2.26 per night bed & breakfast and can have dinner, bed & breakfast for £2.97. Preferable to book in advance but you can also book on the spot at the reception centre. Very few restrictions.

LEONARD HORNER HALL, 19 Great King Street (556 2698 or 556 2680). Open July to September for students and non-students, with 64 beds available in single, double and sharing rooms (for up to 4 people). Charges are £1.60 (single room) and £1.50 (sharing)—both bed and breakfast. Dinner by arrangement, 40p. No bookings after 19.00. Usually well booked up in advance but might have some space available.

BRYSON HOUSE, 5 Drummond Place (556 4801). Same charges and similar amenities to Leonard Horner Hall.

CARLYLE HOSTEL, East Suffolk Road (667 1564 or 667 2262). Students and non-students. Bed & breakfast £1.65; dinner, bed & breakfast £2.25. Again only in the summer months. Book in advance.

EDINBURGH HOSTEL, 8 Regent Terrace (556 7851). Open July 1st to September 8th. Male and female dormitories—90p bed & breakfast (15 beds in each). Also double, triple and four-bedded rooms at £1.20 bed & breakfast. Unlike most other hostels it's open all day.

THE SCOTTISH YOUTH HOSTEL ASSOCIATION has four hostels in Edinburgh, but a membership card is a must (you can join at any hostel). All of them cater for both sexes (separately) and offer dormitory accommodation. The main centre is at 8 Bruntsfield Crescent (447 2464), open 07.00-11.00 and 16.00-23.45. The others are at 13 Eglinton Crescent (which also provides meals), and the Merchiston Boys Club in Watson Crescent and the Ramsay Technical Institute, Inchview Terrace, Portobello (669 3580). Beware of regulations, e.g. no entry after 23.45, no smoking in dormitories etc. It's cheap, though, and allows you to cook for yourself.

YMCA HOSTELS accept males and females. The hostel at 12 Rothesay Place (225 2134) also takes couples and families and provides single, twin and shared rooms (up to 4 people). You don't have to be a member for a temporary stay. Bed & breakfast charges at Rothesay Place vary from £1.43 for a shared room to £1.65 for a single. Weekly partial board (bed, breakfast & dinner) ranges from £10.50-£12 (not including VAT). Regulations are fairly lax. If you can't get in there, try the YMCA hostel at St. Andrews St. (556 4303) where there is dormitory accommodation with breakfast for around £1 a night.

The YWCA HOSTEL, 14 Coates Crescent (225 3771) takes females only. Most of its places are filled by Edinburgh residents( students, nurses and working girls). Accommodation here is mostly shared rooms and cubicles and charges vary from £10-£12 per week (inclusive of VAT). If restrictions annoy you it's best to steer clear of here: although they do issue late keys (50p deposit), 'lights out' is 23.00, and residents under 18 are only permitted late keys twice a week. All very proper. As one resident put it, "We still respect the Sabbath here".

# Hotels, Guest Houses and Private Houses

### Hotels:

If you can afford this kind of thing (a minimum of £1.50 bed and breakfast during the summer season) a full list is available at 1 Cockburn Street.

The following four places all charge less than £1.50.

ASHLYN HOTEL, 42 Inverleith Row (552 2954)

BELMONT HOTEL, 10 Carlton Terrace
METROPOLE HOTEL, 6 Mayfield Gdns. (667 3587).
STUART HOTEL, 4 Palmerston Rd. (667 2715)

Don't expect too much from any hotel though; probably you can hope for clean sheets, a wash basin, lighting inclusive and a sitting room with TV. A few also supply a baby-sitting service, reductions, for kids and additional cheap meals. With all hotels, especially the smaller, cheaper ones, it's better to book in advance. For neat hotels the winter rates are between 10 and 50% lower. None of the prices quoted in the Edinburgh Tourist Accommodation Register include VAT.

### Guest Houses:

The Tourist Accommodation Register lists around 150—which tend to be slightly cheaper than registered hotels. This list is more lightly to be supplemented by scanning the Evening News, Scotsman and newsagents' windows.

### Private Houses:

Even cheaper still. About 90 are registered with the Tourist Accommodation Service but many are only signified by a notice in the window. Facilities are less comprehensive than in hotels but there are official minimum standards which must be maintained.

## Camping and Caravans

There are no free or really central campsites in Edinburgh. Average charges are around 50p for a caravan and 20-40p for a tent (depending on the size). You can also expect adequate toilets, shower rooms, and a general grocery shop on each. Best are at the Municipal site at Muirhouse (225 2424) and the Little France site, Old Dalkeith Rd. (667 4742), both open in the summer months only.

## Keeping Clean

### Hot Baths

All of the public baths in Edinburgh—with the exception of the Portobello outdoor pool—provide hot baths of a high standard, while two, Portobello (indoor) and Warrender, also provide the more exotic Turkish and aerotone. There is a fixed charge for hot baths in each of them—

| Bath | Towel | Soap | Shampoo | Bath cubes |
|------|-------|------|---------|------------|
| 11p | 4p-25p deposit | 1p | 3p | 1½p |

There's some variation as to when they're open for hot baths, so best check first. The various public baths are—

DALRY, Caledonian Cres. (337 3915)
GLENOGLE, Glenogle Rd. (332 5508)
INFIRMARY ST. (556 5006)
LEITH, Junction Pl. (554 1953)
PORTOBELLO (indoor), Bellfield St. (669 2189)
WARRENDER, Thirlestane St. (447 2780)

It's often cheaper, though, just to have a shower and a swim—admission to any of the above pools costs 11p, 5p for kids.

## A free Wash

Depending on your nerve, a free bath or shower can be had. Easiest place is any student hostel or hall of residence. Youth and tourist hostels again are easier, just get to know someone staying there. Crashing hotel bathrooms is slightly more difficult. Appearance is important. Sit in the lobby (if asked you're waiting for somebody) until reception is busy, then walk quickly upstairs or into the lift. Even the plushest hotels usually have at least one 'public' bathroom on each floor. Alternatively, look and act as if you have full rights to be there and stroll proudly past reception.

If you only want a quick wash in a washhand basin, things are easier still. Apart from public conveniences (usually either inadequate or cost a few pence), pubs, cafes and restaurants usually provide washing facilities. Best look out for places where the toilets are separated from the rest of the establishment i.e. so that you don't have to walk through the bar or the restaurant to get to the loo. Otherwise try hostels and hotel bogs.

### Washing Clothes

There are roughly 50 Launderettes with coin-operated washing machines and driers in Edinburgh. The average charge is about 15p for a 9 lb. load. Most launderettes will

62

offer service washes, some charging an extra 5p for this if they're busy, others do it free. For a full list check the yellow pages at the back of a phone book.

For the best deal and a more human atmosphere, try any of Edinburgh Corporation's public wash-houses. Best are Leith at Bonnington Row (554 1953) and Murdoch Ter. (229 1682). Besides being the only two with washing machines, these have the added attraction of including drying in the price— usually 27p for a 15 lb.load. In the older ones washing stalls will cost you 15p for up to 2 hours. Even cheaper of course is to do it yourself free at any student hall of residence or youth hostel.

## Toilets

The standard of public loos in Edinburgh is about the same as any other city in Britain—bad. The Cleansing Department boasts that it provides 39 Gents' and 32 Ladies'. However, of the 39 conveniences set aside for the male Edinburgher, only four are open day and night—

REGISTER (West Register St.)
WEST END (in Princes St. Gdns. opp. Charlotte St.)
ALBERT ST. at Leith Walk
GORGIE RD. at Poole's Roxy

The last three of these are urinals only.

Women are even worse off, only one 24-hour loo for them—West End (Princes St. Gardens). Significantly, the Corporation sees fit to open a further toilet at Castle Terr. Car Park (male and female) during the Festival each year. There is no evidence to show that this move is in any way related to the amount of crap produced each year at the time.

In case of emergency—try the nearest pub, hotel or friendly looking house.

# and on the seventh day..

## SUNDAY

O Knox he was a bad man
he split the Scottish mind.
The one half he made cruel
and the other half unkind.
**ALAN JACKSON**

"Paradoxical as it may seem to you, O Lord..." Sunday in Edinburgh like that Highland Minister's prayer, remains a mass of contradictions. Since John Knox Sunday has the reputation of being a non-scene, a supposedly strict day of rest behind closed doors and minds. In fact for most people Sunday is "The Sunday Post" and the "News of the World".

Basic services are somewhat limited: Sunday bus services are denoted by a circle round the route numbers at stops, operating on a limited timetable, and train services, other than the Edinburgh—Glasgow line (hourly on the half hour) are spasmodic. Details from Waverley Station (556 2394). Post Offices are not open. Cashing cheques is possible only at hotels and shops (few in number) and even then only with a bankers card. Only the bank at Turnhouse Airport (08.30—13.30) will change money and cash cheques.

Doctors usually alternate in taking calls with the help of the GPO's redirection service. BOOTS Chemist, Shandwick Pl. is open (11.00—20.00), otherwise the hospitals and the Dental Hospital, 31 Chambers St. (225 5261).

Recently a Sunday market has opened at Powderhall Stadium car park. Nice material and lots of other junk but no food stalls.

However in most areas several shops open till lunch time selling rolls, newspapers, groceries and milk—sadly at higher Sunday prices. Stalls at Waverley Station and St. Andrew Bus Station provide papers, magazines, cigarettes and confectionery. LURIE'S, Buccleuch St., is one of few butchers open, till 13.00. Some shops, listed below, remain open on Sunday afternoons.

LARDER, 5 Raeburn Pl.—till 22.00—groceries, not cheap.
MACE, 11 Raeburn Pl.—fruit and groceries.
MARGARET'S MINI MARKET, Henderson Row. 07.30—20.00. Nice delicatessen and grocer.
DAIRY, 48 St. Patricks Sq. Dairy and grocer—open till 19.30.
DELICACIES CENTRE, 7 Barony St. Very nice Polish delicatessen.
EDINBURGH CHINESE CO., Dublin St. Nice Chinese delicatessen.
HONG KONG STORE, Morrison St.
FINLAY'S, Morrison St. Papers and provisions.
FOOD FOR CASH, Dundas St./Henderson Row.
GENERAL GROCERY, foot of Broughton St.
GENERAL STORE, head of Lawnmarket. Till 13.30.
CURRIES, 5a Sciennes. Groceries.
BUCKIE, 17 Causewayside. General provisions.
ASIAN STORES, 45 Clerk St. Cheap groceries.
THE ORIENT, Argyle Pl. Asian and conventional provisions.
CAPALDI'S, 164 Bruntsfield Pl.
GROCER, 176 Morningside Rd. Till 20.00
GERRY'S, 21 Grassmarket. 06.00—23.00.
PHILLIPS, 45 Blackfriars St. Open to 01.00.
SUNRISE GROCERS, 225 Dalry Rd. Open to 23.00.
GENERAL STORE, 3 Leamington Terr.
KLEINBERG, Jewish baker, 6 am—1 pm, nice shop.

# EATING

Finding a place open is often an achievement in itself. The ubiquitous chip shop can be a life saver and most districts have one or two open on a Sunday. There are however several good restaurants where eating out can compensate for the lack of fun elsewhere—

HOUSTON HOUSE, Uphall (Broxburn 3831). Open to 21.00, £1—1.75. Several miles out but if you're on wheels, good value.
SORRENTO, 15 Albert Pl. (554 7282). 17.30—midnight. £1.50.
HAWES INN, by Forth Bridges (Queensferry 215). Open to 21.45. Approx. £2. Bus to the Forth Bridge and walk down. Chinese approx. £1.
OPEN ARMS, Dirleton (Dirleton 241). 12.30—14.00, 19.00—21.30. Near North Berwick. Upwards of £1.
LOON FUNG, 2 Warriston Pl.—very best Cantonese food, open 12 noon—2 am. Approx. £1.
WELL MET, Gilmore Pl., no. two Chinese in Edinburgh.
SIK TEK FOK, Hanover St. Third of three Cantonese but open till 2 am.

A fair number of medium priced restaurants stay open on Sundays. Here's a selection.

## PRINCES STREET AREA

FARMHOUSE, 75 Hanover St. Average farmhouse-type fare (main meals are good value but soups and sweets expensive).
MILK BAR, S. St. Andrew St. Quite cheap sandwiches and snacks. No cooked food.
CHINESE: DRAGON'S CASTLE, 21 S. Castle St.)—fair reputation. Unexceptional menu at moderate prices. In Hanover St. the GOLDEN GATE (no. 78), HONEYFLOWER (89) and GOLDEN PALACE (97) are much of a Chinese muchness.
WAVERLEY BUFFET and EAST END BUFFET, Waverley Station. Open alternate Sundays, standard British Rail.
DEEP SEA II, Union Pl. Reasonable quality, fish and chips.

## HAYMARKET DISTRICT

CAFE HONEYDEW, 1 Grosvenor Cres. Good cafe cuisine at high prices.
MARTY'S GRILL, 29 W. Maitland St. Similar in prices, but not so attractive.
BLUE STAR, 6a W. Maitland St. Expensive Chinese.
STAR OF BENGAL, Haymarket. Expensive curries.
HAYMARKET RESTAURANT, Morrison St. at Haymarket. Fairly dear (by cheap standards).
THE OASIS, Haymarket Terr. Average-priced cafe with wide-ranging menu (steaks/grills/salads/hamburgers).

## HIGH ST./NEWINGTON

POPPIN, Lawnmarket:   good and cheap, and open to 18.00.
CLANSMAN GRIDDLE, 231 High St.    Good but expensive griddle/salads. Open 10.00—22.)).
FARMHOUSE, 130 High St.   Facing the Clansman, and similar. Open 12.00—19.00.
NEWINGTON CAFE, 74 S. Clerk St.  Comprehensive menu.
BRATTISANI'S, 87 Newington Rd.   Average B's—beware queues during University term.
RISI'S, Causewayside—greasy Risi's.
ERASMO'S, Sciennes.  Even greasier, if possible.
CHINA GARDEN, 28 Clerk St. (667 8276).  17.30—23.00, small portions.

## MEADOWS AREA

ROSSI'S BUFFET,Morningside Rd.  Carry-out sandwiches, ice cream.
CANDY BOX, Morningside Rd.  Average menu.
DIMARCO'S, Marchmont Rd.  Only cafe in the area.
COPPER KETTLE, Bruntsfield Pl.  Good cafe, ice cream.
VJ'S PLACE, Bruntsfield Pl.  Salads/hot snacks/grills.
GLOBETROTTER, Bruntsfield Pl.  Ambitious menu—scampi/curries/omelettes/trout/grills—prices to match.
INTERNATIONAL, Gilmore Pl.  Fish/chicken bar.

# ENTERTAINMENT

Cinemas open on Sunday on a rota basis, either showing the new weekly programme or with a special Sunday bill (usually 19.30), Edinburgh University Film Society runs weekly showings in the Odeon, S. Clerk St. from 19.30. The Traverse Theatre, Grassmarket, stages performances at 19.30 (periodically 22.30) with restaurant open 18.00—23.00 and bar 19.00—22.00.

Art galleries and museums, covered in 'Kultur' section, are open after 14.00 on Sundays—as yet free; entertainment is promised on Princes St. at the Speakers' Corner where political and religious groups congregate or at the Bandstand where there are weekly concerts.  Even sport is now generally available on Sundays.

# DRINKING

No pubs are open on Sundays in Scotland, moreover it is illegal to buy carry-outs, so drinking is restricted to hotels with 7 day licences, between the hours of 12.30—14.30, 18.30—22.00.  Some of the more pleasant, though still not cheap drinking places are:

The COUNTY HOTEL, Abercromby Pl., ADELPHI, Cockburn St., HOWARD HOTEL, Gt. King St., GLENCAIRN HOTEL, Royal Circus, RAEBURN HOUSE, Raeburn Pl., PEACOCK HOTEL, Newhaven, COMMODORE, Marine Drive, BUCKINGHAM, Buckingham Terr.,MURRAYFIELD HOTEL,Corstorphine Rd.,GROSVENOR CENTRE, Grosvenor Pl., RUTLAND, West End, BRUNTSFIELD, Bruntsfield Pl., IONA, Whitehouse Loan, MINTO, Minto St., PARK ROYAL, Royal Terr.

# RELIGION

### PERFECT

**when a christian hits the ground
he splits in two**

**one half is rotten
and so's the other**
ALAN JACKSON

Religion is traditionally supposed to be the hub of the Edinburgh Sunday. Apart from the traditional church-goers, you'll find that religion has little to do with Sunday and Sundays little to do with religion. John Knox would be appalled if he realised how fragmented is the religious establishment in his Reformed City. Starting from the top, places of contact are:

CHURCH OF SCOTLAND, Head Offices, 121 George St. , 226 5722. Bookshop.
THE FREE CHURCH, 15 North Bank St. (226 5286).
BAPTIST MISSIONARY SOCIETY, 4 Melville Terr. (667 8374).
ROMAN CATHOLICS, St. Mary's Cathedral, Broughton St. and "liberated" Catholic Chaplaincy, George Sq. will help.
METHODIST, Central Hall, Tollcross.
SOCIETY OF FRIENDS (Quakers), 28 Stafford St. (225 4825).
SALVATION ARMY, 18 Nicholson St. (667 2394).
THE (MORMON)CHURCH OF JESUS CHRIST OF LATTER DAY SAINTS, 30 Colinton Rd. (337 5825).
ELIM PENTECOSTAL CHURCH, 8 Henderson Terr. (337 3684).
EPISCOPAL, West End Cathedral (St. Mary's), Palmerston Pl.
SEVENTH DAY ADVENTIST CHURCH, 3 Bristo Pl. (225 3798).
JEHOVAH'S WITNESSES, 556 6318.
CHRISTIAN SCIENCE, Second Church, 9 Young St. (225 7676).
UNITARIAN CHURCH, First Church, Castle Terr.
JEWISH SYNAGOGUE, Salisbury Rd.
THE SIKH TEMPLE, 7 Hope Terr., Leith.

MOSLEM, the University Moslem Association at the Societies Centre, 21 Hill Pl.

TRANSCENDENTAL MEDITATION. Learned over a period of four days, one hour a day; their mentor is the Maharishi Mahesh Yogi. Contact S.I.M.S., 18 Buccleuch Pl. (667 6933). Cost £12 students, £20 others—concessions for those in need.

SUFI. Meditate for progress of the soul to the ideal. Meet every Wednesday, 7.45 pm at 2 Salisbury Rd., Newington (667 5438).

DIVINE LIGHT MISSION. Believes Guru Maharij ji can impart to others the name of God which will give peace to all who know it. Contact the Divine Light Mission, 37 Forrest Rd.

FELLOWSHIP OF RECONCILIATION, St. Cuthberts Hall, Kings Stables Rd. (229 5248). Work for an end to all war and violence and its members are Christian.

INTERNATIONAL SOCIETY FOR KRISHNA CONSCIOUSNESS' Members devote their life to meditation, singing, chanting to awaken the love of God dormant in everyone's heart. They run Radna Krishna Temple, 14 Forrest Rd.

KRISHNA VEDANTA YOGA CENTRE. Concerned with Hatha Yoga; teaches Asana and Pranayama techniques. Contact 24 Shandwich Pl.

BAHA'I FAITH MILLENIAL. Follows the teaching of Baha'u'llah; believes in the unification of mankind. Contact Baha'i Centre, 19a Drumdryan St.

UNIFIED FAMILY. Based on modern teachings from South Korea. Anti-socialist, striving for a god-centred world, created by God-centred families. Contact 25 Royal Terr.

CHRISTIAN COMMUNITY. For "renewal of religion". No official doctrine, the way of life of individual and community considered more important. Contact 21 Napier Rd. (229 8093).

SPIRITUALISM, 28 Stafford St. (225 4825).

EXTRA TERRESTRIAL OBSERVERS: Try the Edinburgh University Astronomical Society, c/o the Mathematical Institute, Chambers St., a possible contact.

SCIENTOLOGY. Ron Hubbard's Institute on South Bridge.

INFO ON THE BLACK ARTS cannot be published under Scots law, but try St. Stephen St. all the same.

# THINGS?

## HIP CLOTHES & GIFTS

Within a capitalist system, there can be no real alternative as far as consumer goods are concerned. But it helps if you know how the system works, then you can turn it to your own advantage. For instance, most trendy boutiques run at least one good line to lure you into the shop — once there, beware of the soft lights and the sweet music.

However, there have been one or two interesting experiments set up in an attempt to bypass the system, e.g. the only two markets in Edinburgh, the one in Cockburn St. and the other in Forrest Rd., where anyone can set up stalls provided they pay weekly rental. Both of these markets have had a noticeable effect in forcing the trendy shops to cut their prices on such things as loons, long skirts and velvets, e.g. St. Stephens St. where the atmosphere is friendly and hassle free. Shops are small and most carry a typical headshop mixture of clothes and accessories. They usually take handmade stuff on sale or return. But at the time of writing, the hip capitalists were moving in and taking over — there are still some good buys to be found if you look carefully.

## MARKETS

GREYFRIARS MARKET, FORREST ROAD—has posters, rings, graphic design, clothes (commercial and second-hand), handmade leather goods, boots and shoes.

COCKBURN STREET — has posters, clothes, Afghan coats (£18) second-hand records, jewellery, handmade boots and shoes.

# HANDMADE

There are a growing number of shops in Edinburgh that are making and selling clothes on the same premises. They will often sell your own handmades for you. These type of shops are well worth visiting, the atmosphere is friendly and if you can't find what you want, they might make it for you.

NUMBER 2, ST. STEPHENS ST. — Everything here handmade, crochet, knitting, and macrame work to order. Really nice kids stuff, smocking and patchwork (pots and wooden spoons too).

MOONDANCE, ST. STEPHENS ST. — All very well handmade clothes, classy stuff, more expensive.

HAND IN HAND, NW CIRCUS PLACE — design and make up clothes from old and new materials. Really nice people.

A BIT ON THE SILLY SIDE, LAURISTON PLACE — Good selection of clothes made by Jenny and her friends, also second-hand trendy gear — cheap.

ANDROMEDA, ROSE STREET — for made to measure or off the peg clothes. Do some nice medieval type designs. Long skirts for £2.50.

# CHARITY SHOPS

While these type of shops ought not to be necessary, since they do exist and provide much needed funds for charity organisations, they are well worth supporting. Apart from that, they often are the cheapest places to shop for second-hand clothes, personal bric a brac and oddments of furniture.

MARGARET TUDOR ROSE SHOP, LAURISTON PLACE — Funds for Old Peoples Welfare Council of Edinburgh and Leith. Second-hand clothes and unusual bric a brac.

STOCKBRIDGE HOUSE SHOP, 22 BRUNTSFIELD PLACE — Funds for Old Folks Home. Buys and sells second-hand clothes.

SHELTER SHOP, CAUSEWAYSIDE — sells everything from baby clothes to budgie cages. Nice Pottery.

OXFAM SHOP, 10 BRUNTSFIELD PLACE — Cheapest place for second-hand clothes.

NEARLY NEW, CAUSEWAYSIDE, YMCA SHOP — Good quality clothes at OK prices.

YWCA CLEARANCE CENTRE, 68 HENDERSON ROW — Ladies' clothes, shoes, handbags.

BEAUTY WITHOUT CRUELTY, W. NICHOLSON STREET — For animal lovers. Sells just what the name suggests plus a few (new) gift type things.

ANIMAL DISPENSARY, GEORGE IV BRIDGE — provides funds to pay vets fees for those animals that can't afford them. Sells a lot of second-hand baby clothes, toys and things.

EX TOGS, 4 GRANGE ROAD — Money for . . . . . . .
Mostly ladies clothes.

(NB. Charity Shop stocks always need replenishing)

## TRENDY BOUTIQUES

Concentrate on their cheap lines, be careful of the rest. Means a lot of foot work but worth it. Cheapest for everything places are usually the shops scattered throughout the city selling Eastern and Indian gear — cheapest that is for the buyer. Not a place to shop for those with ideological objections to buying the produce of the exploited people of the Third World. The profit margins for these set-ups are much higher than those of the conventional chain stores.

BUZZ, ROSE STREET — Good for tee shirts. New French Sun Sand range. Worth a visit for the music alone. Friendly place, ask for Nigel.

NICARS, ST. MARYS ST — for cheap loons £2.

KOOLMINI, 248 CANONGATE — Cheese cloth shirts (£3.25). Cheese cloth used to be the cheapest thing on the market. Extra charge must cover the carriage cost from India?? Velvet Loons.

SUMAR KUMAR, ST. STEPHENS ST. — Mainly Indian clothes. Usual Kaftans £3.50. Also nice silver jewellery.

HEADQUARTERS, Sth. COLLEGE ST. — Clothes, mainly Indian, chillums, skins and joss. Nice lights and records show in the cellar.

FORBIDDEN FRUIT, ST. STEPHENS ST. — Small company with factory and four shops in London. Only one branch in Scotland. Mainly indian type stuff. Some nice skirts, from £2.50.

## FOR SOMETHING SPECIAL

FORUM, Sth. COLLEGE ST. & ROSE ST. — the 'in' shop for chicks usually first with fashion. Prices high.

CAMPUS, GRASSMARKET — Prices even higher, exclusive designs.

THE GREAT WESTERN TRADING CO., COCKBURN ST. — denim for all. This is the place to buy that faded, frayed and patched denim jeans/jacket/waistcoat/hat/bag you've always wanted. Jackets at £7.50.

## FOOTGEAR

Both COCKBURN ST. MARKET and GREYFRIARS MARKET

sell handmade boots and clogs.

PIGGIES, Sth CLERK ST. — Large selection of boots and clogs, all handmade, beautiful colours. £4.50 (also for cheapest loons at £1.99).

JACKI, 20A DUNDAS ST. — Means clogs, black, sizes 8-11 for £3.50. Also suede sandals — female.

SCHOLL SHOP, CASTLE ST. — for the whole Scholl range and repairs. But these can sometimes be found selling cheaper as special lines in small chemists like Spense of Newington Road, also try 'Boots'.

PIU BELLA, St. MARY ST. & KOOLMINI, Canongate for sandals.

FOR REPAIRS:

TIMPSONS do a cheap 'while you wait' repair service. Try PLEN-DERLEITH, NICHOLSON St. for anything tricky. If you explain exactly what you want done, they'll be OK.

P.S. Try bare feet and blue nail varnish or a morrocan henna dye. It's cheaper and less of a hassle. Makes for interesting conversation.

## SECOND-HAND CLOTHES

For best and cheapest places see also Charity shops.

WORLDLY GOODS, St. Stephen St.—very good for shawls, velvet, suede, fur coats. Have a rummage through their cheap boxes — great fun.

CAUSEWAYSIDE SALEROOM — Gent's clothes mainly. Bought and sold.

BRUNTSFIELD THRIFT SHOP, 6 BRUNTSFIELD PLACE — Ladies clothes mainly, occasionally fur coats.

MADAME DOUBTFIRES, S.E. CIRCUS PLACE — Don't be deterred by the smell, you never know what you might find.

CLOTHES PEG, 202 LEITH WALK — First to make second-hand clothes respectable.

THE NEXT-TO-NEW SHOP in COMISTON ROAD, sells just about everything, junk, antiques, clothes for all ages — pediatric to geriatric. The owner Helen Sprott is never quite sure what she's got so rummage around — prices are low.

HIRE — Theatrical clothes hire — or just for fun — Mutrie, Broughton Street.

FREE CLOTHES — Salvation Army. If you are really destitute they have a supply of free clothes (which always needs replenished) 5 GRASSMARKET for women, THE PLEASANCE for men.

## BASIC INFO ON BASIC CLOTHES

Best areas for this type of stuff, Leith Walk or Lothian Road.

LEITH ARMY STORES, 10 BRUNSWICK PLACE — the usual army surplus.

NORTHERN SUPPLIES STORE, 359 LEITH WALK. OK Swedish coats and camping gear.

WAVERLEY TAILORING CO., EARL GREY ST. & LOTHIAN RD. for cheap jeans.

COWANS TAILORING LOTHIAN RD. & Sth. BRIDGE — big jean selection.

BURROWS SHOPS scattered across the city sell cheap woollens, M. & S. rjects, kids clothes and duffle coats.

HEWITTS OF EDINBURGH, TEVIOT ROW — for jeans and overalls.

# PERSONAL GIFTS & THINGS

Try Charity shops and second-hand junk shops for unusual gifts. Or make your own. Visit STRATA St. Stephens St. for stones, take your own to be polished. Also provide settings in stailess steel or silver.

STUDIO ONE, STAFFORD ST. — Wide range of stuff at various prices.

TOWN CHOICE, CANONGATE — Cheapest in the High St.

EASTERN CRAFTS, CANONGATE — The original Indian craft shop in Edinburgh.

ROMULUS, ROSE ST. — for expensive stuffed toys and cuddly things.

PIU BELLA, ST. MARY'S ST. for hats and bags.

Cheap canvas bags and wickerwork baskets from TIMPSONS, NICHOLSON ST.

McANNE, ROSE ST. — Magnificent range of chess pieces and boards.

CARBERRY CANDLES, Musselburgh, materials cheap to make your own.

# TOILETRY

BOOTS are hard to beat.

TALK OF THE TOWN, 7 HOME ST., TOLLCROSS — for cut price toiletries.

HEPBURNS, of Sth. CLERK ST. for cut price toiletries.

BEAUTY WITHOUT CRUELTY, — products contain no animal oils, etc.

NAPIERS, BRISTO ST. — stock both their own herbal stuff and the Swiss Valeda range.

JUST US, ROSE ST., — meadow herb beauty products.

PIU BELLA, St. Mary's St. — is the only place in Edinburgh to have Culpepper products. Reckoned to be the best herbal stuff but not the cheapest around.

PATONS, Level St., Tollcross — Leichner stage make up.

## MAKE YOUR OWN CLOTHES

**Machines and Materials** — Although it is cheaper to sew by hand, it's better and faster if you can have the use of a machine. You can usually pick up an old treadle or hand-machine at auctions or in junk shops for about £5. Singer have a policy of buying up all their old machines so these are becoming more difficult to find.

NEWARK'S, 2 GILLESPIE PLACE — have a lot of old machines, slightly more expensive but guaranteed to work. They will also fit machines with electric motors for £8.50 — they collect the machine fit it and deliver it within three days.

THE SINGER SHOP, PRINCES STREET — sells new and revamped models, also the best place for machine accessories.

RAPIDE ELECTRIC, NICHOLSON ST. — have second-hand electric machines.

There is no place in Edinburgh that hires out machines but if you are lucky enough to get hold of a student card, then you can have the use of a machine in the Chambers St. Union (open term time only). Pollock Halls residents also have the use of electric machines, but these have to be booked.

**Paper Patterns** — tend to be very expensive. It's best to get a good basic pattern and adapt it or make your own ones. Use masking tape and old newspaper, or better still, see if you can persuade Scotsman Publications (Market St. entrance) to let you have the end of the roll. Ask nicely and be sure to return the inside tubing.

THE SILK SHOP, FREDERICK ST. — has a wide selection of everything for dressmaking — mostly uninspired stuff.

BRACKEN TEXTILES, SHANDWICK PLACE — The material is more accessible and the atmosphere less of a hassle. Good for cottons and towelling.

JENNERS, PRINCES ST. — for the Liberty range of Fabrics. Expensive — wait until sale time.

HAND IN HAND, N.W. CIRCUS PLACE — small range of cheap colourful indian cottons and ginghams. Also old lace and buttons.

PATRICK THOMPSONS, THE BRIDGES — has the best haberdashery department. Lots of nice ribbons and trimmings.

SMITHS, FREDERICK ST. — have fantastic sales. Really good for embroidery thread, tapestry wool, canvas and zips. Its a good idea to buy here in bulk at sale time. Also a good selection of knitting patterns but the wool is expensive.

Best buy in wool is to get a cone either from one of the BURROWS shops or from JASPERS, LEVEN ST. TOLLCROSS. Averages out about 4p an ounce.

MARGARET TUDOR ROSE SHOP, LAURISTON PLACE, — sell knitting needles and also try jumble sales.

### Nothing

Nothing in my woman's head
didn't worry about that
Took her into C and A's
and bought her a great big purple woolly hat.
ALAN JACKSON

## BOOKS

Edinburgh is well provided with both first and second-hand bookshops, nearly all centrally located. All operate within the existing laws concerning stocking and the selling of books—some adding extra censorship refinements of their own. This means that many books available overseas are not available here, and secondly that though some books do have copyright arrangements, some bookshops refuse to stock them because they consider them undesirable (usually for political reasons).

BETTER BOOKS, Forrest Rd. is the best bookshop in Edinburgh both for traditional books, and for a satisfactory selection of the smaller more independent and radical publications (i.e. cinema, theatre, arts, folk law, sex, Politics).

Though for a more comprehensive range one would need to go to bookshops further afield (e.g. Compendium Books, London)

BAUERMEISTER, George IV Bridge, traditional stock, strong on continental books, paperbacks, social science texts, Scottishery, continental newspapers and magazines.

JAMES THINS. The largest bookshop with 4 branches. Their main shop in South Bridge stocking scientific, languages, school and university books, stationery, art novels, paperbacks, and a good childrens department as well as small records dept, and some secondhand and theological book in basement. The 2 shops in Buccleuch St. stock social science, art, paperbacks and stationary,& they have a third shop at Edinburgh University Kings Buildings, specialising in scientific texts.

Then there are the specialist bookshops:

Medical texts: DONALD FERRIER, Teviot Pl. (who also runs an excellent medical lending library).

Veterinary texts: CAIRN'S VET. BOOKSHOP, Causewayside.

Legal & Accounting texts: GREEN'S, High Street.

Gout Publications: The GOVERNMENT BOOKSHOP, Castle Street.

And by the way you can open charge accounts at most shops.

There is one remainder bookshop in Edinburgh at Greyfriars Bobby (George IV Bridge). It contains a varied stock of new books at greatly undercut prices. Ask for free latest list of all books remaindered.

## SELL YOUR OWN BOOKS

The BOOKS EXCHANGE, 138 Dundas St. give you 25% face value of book and sell if for 50% face value. The Bookcellar and David Balfour both have paperbacks at about two-thirds or less of face value. There are a large number of branches of Bobbie's Bookshop who will buy or take them in part exchange.

## SECOND HAND BOOKS

Particularly university books at the SRC Book Exchange, Chambers St. Thins and Baxendine also buy university books for half price when in the mood.

## STATIONERY

Cheap and good selection at SRC shops in Chambers St. and David Hume Tower, Buccleuch Pl. or Brown of the Mound.

# RECORDS

Most of the record shops have good selections of current LP's of all types. Among the big shops, three stand out. Firstly, if you're into classical music, then the shop for you is RAE MACINTOSH of Queensferry St. Apart from Kultur, the shops with the best selection for rock, west coast, country, folk, jazz, blues and a wide selection of imports is BRUCE'S, 79 Rose St. and VIRGIN, Thistle St., who do discounts.

Of the other shops with good stocks and cheaper than average prices, the best for second hand and greatly reduced records, popular or classical, is the RECORD EXCHANGE in South Clerk St. Their second hand records range from 50p upwards, with certain new records at £1.65 or less. Also many classical records, many greatly reduced. There is even a cut-price 45 section with records at 20p, including many obscure American soul discs.

HEADQUARTERS in S. College St. specialise in west coast sounds, though they also have lots of others. Records sell up to 36p below retail; second hand records from 30p to £1.50—75, and they don't hassle you into buying anything.

Some imports and a nice shop with nice people.

Also worth a mention are BANDPARTS of 235 Leith Walk and 27 Antigua St., GREYFRIARS RECORD EXCHANGE Forrest Rd. (purely second hand) and SWEET INSPIRATION, Morrison St.

LISTENING: By far the nicest place is HEADQUARTERS, which has not only seats and stereo phones, but also a lightshow. BRUCE'S and STUDIO ONE also have headphones but RAE MACINTOSH and the RECORD EXCHANGE still have the old booths. For free sounds without buying, HQ and BRUCE'S won't hassle.

MUSICAL INSTRUMENTS: RAE MACINTOSH, Queensferry St., GORDON SIMPSONS, 6 Stafford St. and PETE SEATONS, 18 Hope Park Terr. have most music accessories, but the music stall in GREYFRIARS MARKET, Forrest Rd. might be the best place to buy/sell/advertise anything unusual. MESSRS. ROSS—junior and senior—in GLENN'S bagpipe shop in the Lawnmarket can—and will, when in the mood—tell you more about bagpipes than you believed possible. If you are the right sort of person they might even sell you a set.

## FLAT THINGS

FREE: Dustbins can furnish your entire flat. In two weeks we found a fireside chair, a full length mirror, 2 tables, a TV kitchen chairs, books and a roofrack. Get to know your local bin night, but remember it's illegal! Get on good terms with your dustman: for a small consideration he can supply anything under the sun.

Another source of very cheap furniture can be jumble sales, information from Friday's **Evening News**. If even their prices are too high, at the end of sales organisers will practically pay you to remove what is left—oblige them. The same goes for the lane sales, Thistle St. where unsold furniture is simply broken up. Free carpeting can be made up from surplus 'swatches' from carpet stores.

## SECOND HAND AUCTIONS

For the very cheapest furniture, Lyon & Turnbull lane sales in Thistle St.Lane, Tuesday and Fridays at 11.00. For slightly more expensive, but still basic furniture, Dowells in Merchiston Rd. on Wednesdays at 11.00. Patersons, Central Auction Rooms, 1 Broughton Pl. Tollcross also have cheap furniture at 12.00 on Thursdays, but their forte is cookers, fridges, TV's and carpets from 14.00 onwards. Another good auction for electrical goods, cameras and basic household goods is Aitken & Dodds, Broughton St., viewing and sales times from the Evening News, usually 12.00 on Tuesdays. For details of their more expensive sales phone 225 2266 Dowells, 225 4627 Lyon and Turnbulls.

## SECOND HAND STORES

These vary from junk to 'antique' and are generally more expensive than sales. At the junk end, McEwan's, 43 Brunswick Rd. sells everything from golf clubs to silver. Barry's at 213 High St. is an amazing basement gloryhole; another unbelievable basement is Greig, 119 Henderson Row and Madame Virtue, Henderson Row.

Many second hand shops sell 10-year old modern (sic) furniture at inflated prices, avoid them.

You won't get a bargain at an antique shop unless you know more about it than the seller. Even so it can be fun browsing so here are the best areas.

The most central, most tourist orientated and therefore the most expensive area is around the Grassmarket, the further from Victoria St. the cheaper the shops. Another area is Stockbridge with a cluster of shops in N.W. Circus Pl., Deanhaugh St. and St. Stephen St.

SECOND-HAND FURNITURE, unusual sources: Get ex-capt.'s cabin from Thomas Ward (Inverkeithing 3261) or Jas. White (Inverkeithing 3441). Shipbreakers, everything from a needle to an anchor. Similarly John Hunter Demolition Merchants, 142 Duddingston Rd. West (661 1242) have lots of unusual stuff. Sam Burns junkyard, Prestonpans is full of furniture, looks cheap but isn't always, occasional weird bargains. Aircraft seats from BEA, Heathrow—£7—10 double seat.

NEW FURNITURE: Invariably a rip-off but some fun things we found were water beds, Mushroom, Lauriston Pl. (£40 with frame); Moondance, St. Stephen St. with beautiful handmade things and Airlux in Hanover St. for sophisticated inflatable furniture (not joint-proof). Basketwork: Royal Blind Asylum, 53 George St. and Bruntsfield Pl.

A Consumer Club (225 3909) card can save 10—20% in many shops.

NEW ELECTRICAL: The cheapest for Hifi, TV, fridges etc. is Comet, Newhaven Rd. (see Evening News for ad). To go anywhere else is crazy. For small electrical fitments, plugs etc. the All Electric Shop, Tollcross is cheap and seems to have every electrical gadget ever made. Rapide Electric at 1 St. Patrick St. stock the cheapest spot-lamp bulbs. S.E. Oriel Display, Howe St., the cheapest spot fittings.

SECOND-HAND ELECTRICAL: See auctions above and City TV, 85 Morrison St., 29 Cockburn St. Adams (pawn saleroom), 4 High Riggs, and SHC, 73 St. Leonard St. have radios, tape recorders, cameras, etc.

**FLOORS:** Sanding—see "Bricks and Things" section. Lino: Peter Miller, 24 Union Pl. and Cockburn Linoleum Warehouse are reasonable (the latter have cheap marim rugs and sisal matting). Carpets, new: Lyon & Turnbull, George St. carpet sales 4 times a year, and 1 Brougham Pl. saleroom. Tayweave-Sidlaw Industries, Meadowsite, Dundee (0382-23161) have 'Tayweave' carpeting (92p per sq. yard) and new sisal matting, very tough (66p a sq. yard, 108 ins. wide). NB ex-exhibit sisal-matting from Sapphire Carpets Ltd., London— even cheaper.

**CHRISTMAS DECORATIONS:** Free from dairies—the silver foil from milk bottle tops—really beautiful— ask nicely.

**WALLS:** The cheapest way to transform a room is a coat of paint, from Hays, 52 Great Junction St., Leith (e.g. 70p/5 litres of paint), Roche, Grindlay St. who give 33½% off Magicoat, or Woolworths, a 'Which' best buy.

**HARDWARE:** Forrest's, 60 Newington Rd. has heaps of hardware everywhere, things unobtainable elsewhere. Polythene buckets etc. from Bargain Centre, Lothian St. Parkers, Nicholson St. Cutlery, the lane sales again or new from Dutch House, Marshall St. Tools, cheap from Woolworths, sophisticated from Ferrier and Alston, 48—50 George IV Bridge, or Murrays Tool Store, Haymarket. Keys: Maclarens, 29 Bread St. are the locksmiths in Edinburgh. Brushes: Cresser, 40 Victoria St.

## MAKE YOUR OWN FURNITURE

**FREE:** James Grant East (Gardener Pl.) for old cardboard display tubing (30 ins. diameter); Reid Corrugated for cardboard boxes— makes stools, chairs, shelves, etc. Wooden boxes from Robt. Lamb, Beaverhall (556 4148) to order—shelving or storage. Cork flooring (3/1 ft. x ½ in.), 20p per tile and cork wall tiles (£1.80—3.00 sq. yard) from Bathgate Cork Co., 39 Cumberland St. They also sell expanded polystyrene granules (4 cu. ft., 37p a bag) and beads (8 cu. ft., £4), for floor cushions,and seat sacks. Foam blocks (£1 per cu. ft.) and foam chips (£4 for 40 lbs.) from the Sleep Shop, 30 Raeburn Pl.

**TEXTILES:** Sidlaw Industries Ltd., Denburn Works, Brechin (Mr. Robertson) have off cuts for curtains, cushions etc. Ring Brechin 2253. Tay Textiles, Park Mill, Dundee (0382-23100) have hessian, 18p per sq. yd., 40 ins. wide, all colours, sacking—soft sacking for walls, furniture etc. (stronger than hessian) undyed, 15p per sq. yd. Huge range. (Also hessian from John Barry, 69 Bonnington Rd., Edinburgh. See also 'Make Your Own Clothes' above.)

## BRICKS AND THINGS

If you want to do your own building or improving, buy cheap timber, bricks, tiles or anything from a demolition contractor:

John Hunter, 142 Duddingston Rd. West (661 1242); C. Brand, 135 Constitution St. (554 5801).

# Improving your Home

You can get money from the government to improve your home in two ways, for repairs to the house to bring it up to a fit level (all mod.cons). The Direct Improvement Grant, from the Corporation Housing Department amounts to 75% of the cost of work completed before July 31st 1974. Do the repairs yourself or with a skilled friend and charge the Corporation. If your ideas are on a higher plane there are various combinations of financial schemes whereby the Government can arrange loans to organised associations to purchase, improve and lease at low rent cheap houses. For the full details on the conditions for recognition as an Association and the various loan schemes available see the Scottish Development Board, 83 Princes Street. Remember, block buying is cheaper.

## FOR PLANT HIRE

Thomson Plant Hire—e.g. sanders £6/day, £14/week. 125 Fountainbridge; Construction Tools (Electric), 26 Ballantyne Rd., Edinburgh 6 (554 6675)—also have sanders.

For new materials, don't go to the Do-It-Yourself shops, go to a builders merchant.

J. Lawson, 131 Fountainbridge (229 1294) are cheapest for most things.

New wood from Garland & Rodgers, Baltic St., Leith. For the determined do-it-yourself shopper, Lawson, in Lady Lawson St., are the largest and often the cheapest.

## MAINTENANCE

EMERGENCIES: The Scottish Gas Board can be reached at 556 2468, the South of Scotland Electricity Board at 229 7311 or 229 2444 outside office hours, and the Water Board at 226 3371 (661 2622 outwith office hours). In an emergency, for corporation property phone 225 2424, otherwise the police have a list of 24 hr. tradesmen.

For less urgent work and if you can't do the job yourself, try the classified advertisements in the Evening News. Get as many estimates as possible. Get a contract in writing, for a fixed sum covering materials and labour. The standard SSEB charge is £8 for a power point. Compare against 'Bargains'. Some good contractors we know are listed below, but it pays to ask around.

Plumber: Eddie Moan, Prestonfield Ave. (667 2297).

Builders and Plasterers: John McGachie, 16 Gilmerton Dykes Cres. (664 5339).

# food FOOD **FOOD** f c

Food is rapidly becoming a luxury. The resigned acceptance of general inflation running at 10% a year makes it easy to overlook the startling rise in food prices, which averaged over 16% last year.

By our own survey we found that cheap meats like mince and gigot chops had almost doubled in price over the last year, with other basics like butter and bread not so far behind.

With depressing regularity it is the poorer sections of society that are feeling the worst effects—with an ever larger proportion of a workers wage packet being taken up with the weekly shopping. The Government's half-hearted attempt to redress the poor is spearheaded by the arrival of Butter Tokens, which generously provide ¼lb. of subsidised butter per week. The insidiousness of this system is the need yet again to subject yourself to poverty scrutiny in order to get the food you need. We are being forced to change our eating habits by the price and in some cases unavailability of meat, fish and other features of the standard British meal. Unless, however, you can thrive on a limited diet of cauliflower and cheese (which have been temporarily overlooked in the price rises) the cheapest alternative is to search out, city-wide, the various loss leaders of chain stores, and bargain butchers or grocers. Shopping has become more than ever a strategic battle for survival in the system of free enterprise.

# BEST BUYS CITY WIDE

## BUTCHERS

PATERSONS, 61 Bread St., TAYLORS, 121 West Port and
GRANTS at 15 Bread St. make Tollcross the best place in town for
cheap good butchers. All are good but our favourite is Paterson.
Also WILSON, 19 Grassmarket and the NEWINGTON DELICAT-
ESSEN in W. Preston St. McSWEEN in Bruntsfield makes the best
haggis around.

## BAKERS

Probably the best nation-wide bakers in Edinburgh are CRAW-
FORDS, our favourite local chain is ANDERSONS with 7 shops
scattered about the city. Also worth a special mention is LAW-
RENCE, 5 Yeoman Pl., a small shop that makes positively the best
savoury pies in Edinburgh.

## SPECIALITY BAKERS

JEWISH: KLEINBERG, Crosscauseway—super onion rizo.
ITALIAN BAKER, 49 Elm Row—pizzas, rolls, doughnuts.
HENDERSONS, 1 Brandon Terr.—wholemeal baking.

## FRUIT

There are several cheap chains around the city. LUMSDENS,
SALTMAN and 'AREA NAME' FRUIT BAZAAR are probably the
best. The cheapest area in town is Gorgie Rd. where all three
compete. 'GORGIE' FRUIT BAZAAR, 136 Gorgie Rd. is usually
the cheapest but Saltmans at 179 and Lumsdens at 104 and 213
compete bravely. Alternatively buy from the EDINBURGH
CENTRAL FRUIT MARKET in Slateford.

## GROCERS

BENSONS are cheap grocers with half a dozen shops mainly in the
Leith area. DREVER Foodmarket have shops at 12a Howe St.
and 17 Cadzow Pl. HARCUS at 121 West Port has particularly
cheap cheese and bacon and the ORCHARD at 807 Morningside Rd.
is a good bet for cheese and other dairy foods. COST-U-LESS,
Fountainbridge also good.

## FISH SHOPS

The FISHMONGER at 125 Nicholson St. is the best deal we know.
A. MUNRO, 44 Broughton St. and the PORT SETON FISH SUP-
PLY, 245 Leith Walk are also nice cheap shops. MacMILLANS in
Dundee St. has cheap broken kippers. The best quality retail fish
shops we reckon are THOMSONS with branches at 204 Morrison
At. and 104 St. Johns Rd., Corstorphine.

## VICTUALLERS

For rice, macaroni, lentils, etc:
IAN McCULLOCH, 47 Thistle St. (top flat), a freak who is

cheapest in town. For more variety try THOMSONS, 155 West Port and the MACARONI SHOP, 131 East Crosscauseway. For health foods COCKBURN ST. MARKET is cheapest.

## DELICATESSENS

Our favourite is VALVONA & CROALLA, 19 Elm Row for European stuff, coffee, cheese and wine: for Indian ORIENTAL GROCERS, 25 Argyle Pl. and EURASIAN, 119 Buccleuch St; for Chinese, the HONG KONG STORE, 200 Morrison St.

## BOOZE SHOPS

FAIRBAIRNS, 11 Albert St. (off Leith Walk), AUGUSTUS BARNETT, 12 Hillhouse Rd., Blackhall, ODDBINS, 22 Montague Terr., Goldenacre and SHERS LITTLE SUPERSTORE in Fowler Terr. (off Dundee St.) have the cheapest booze in town. For late night booze see Edinburgh by Starlight.

## SWEETS AND ICE CREAM

WOOLWORTHS, Princes St., have a huge selection. CASEYS, 52 St. Mary's St., the FUDGE HOUSE, 197 Canongate, and 'BOILINGS FOR THE CONNOISSEUR, 28 East Norton St. and the SWEET SHOP at 50 East Crosscauseway all have beautiful homemade sweets. DAILLI MADE, Henderson Row, will sell ice cream by the gallon. The QUERNSTONE, Lochrin Buildings, Tollcross, has a good variety of home made flavoured ice cream, and LUCA'S in Musselburgh is a must for any travellers who happen that way.

## HERB SHOPS

NAPIERS, Bristo Pl., good and cheap; VALVONA, Elm Row—excellent; PIGGIES Boutique, 83 Clerk St. and COCKBURN ST. MARKET stock herbs from Alchemy London—for cooking and herbal highs.

## BEST BUYS—DISTRICT BY DISTRICT

Look at your own area, if you don't find what you want, check best buys city wide and sections dealing with adjacent districts and 'Late Night Edinburgh'.

# CITY CENTRE AND UNIVERSITY

Good shopping area but Nicholson St. is threatened by property developers.

## BUTCHERS

Wm. JACK, 276 Canongate
WILSON, Grassmarket—another cheap, good butcher—recommended.
LURIE-KOSHER Butcher, 30 Buccleuch St. Open Sunday morning.

## BAKERS

KLEINBERG, Jewish baker, super onion rizo, apfelstrudel etc.

Also small delicatessen.
ANDERSON, 5 St. Patrick St.—late night baker and carry-out goodies. Nice people.
ALEX. DICKSON, Chapel St.—Home baker with nice pies.

## FRUIT

The FORREST, George IV Bridge—fruit & pizzas; RANKINS, 79 Nicholson St., nice women; MALCOLM CAMPBELL, 8 St. Patrick St.—cheap loss leaders.

## GROCERS

ARNOTTS Food Hall, Bridges—good selection if not cheap—you can pay by cheque which is useful. McLEANS, 48 Blackfriars St. corner of Cowgate—groceries, magazines, ice cream, tobacco, skins, open till 1:30 am—much beloved by taxi drivers and freaks. THISTLE DAIRY, 11 Thistle St.—carry-out sandwiches, favourite shop for office staff; ASIAN STORES, 45 Clerk St.—Indian foods, cheapish fruit etc. Good for a late night shop; LIPTON'S, 116 Nicholson St.—ask for bacon cut thick as gammon steak. Cheap and tasty.

## FISH

125 NICHOLSON ST, cheap nice shop: kippers 15p, mackerel 18p; GRANTON SEA FOOD, 12 Clerk St.—line-caught fish, mackerel 14p, kippers 30p.

## DELICATESSENS

EURASIAN, 119 Buccleuch St.—good Indian shop. Has packs of Indian savoury lentils and rice flakes, Indian veg. and spices—and instant Indian soups, tinned curries etc. Open till 9:45 six days a week, restaurant attached. FORSYTH'S FOOD MARKET, St. Andrew Sq.—Europeanised delicatessen a la Fortnum's but has some good things. Took over Melroses' last year, also good teas and coffees. Good range of herbs and different types of honey, lots of ethnic sweets; MACARONI SHOP, 31 East Crosscauseway—lots of different types of pastas, cheap. Also has good Parmesan, olive oil, dried herbs, Italian tinned foods etc. Cheap cheese; F & G CONTINENTAL,3 South Clerk St.—this branch sells a lot of Polish food, no prices displayed but a real delicatessen; ARNOTTS Food Hall—good range.

## SPECIALIST SHOPS

HERE'S HEALTH, 2 & 3 Bristo St.—first Health Food Shop in town. Usual prices. NAPIERS HERBALISTS, 1 Teviot Pl.—established 1860, cheapest spices in town and home brew equipment. FUDGE HOUSE, 197 Canongate—unique but no bargains here; 48 EAST CROSSCAUSEWAY—real home made sweets—far out! SWEET SHOP, St. Mary's St.—more far out home made goodies; HEALTH FOOD STORE, 40 Hanover St.—dried fruits, no macro; TOWN & COUNTRY CATERING, William St.—expensive sweets, fresh cream ¼ and ½ pint cartons; MARGARET TUDOR ROSE Shop, Lauriston Pl.—home baked goodies, irregular hours.

## BOOZE

VIN BRU, 40 East Crosscauseway—home brew specialists; PETER GREEN, 88 Nicholson St.—nice people, will deliver, supplies glasses for parties, etc.

# TOLLCROSS

has the cheapest good butchers in town, in Bread St. SHERS for the cheapest booze this side of town, LAWRENCE for the best pies in town, all in all a real good area.

## BUTCHERS

GRANTS, 15 Bread St.—cheap and good; PATTERSONS, 61 Bread St., mince 34p, lamb chops 28p, steak 66p; TAYLOR, 75 Bread St., mince 34p, lamb chops 28p, stewing mutton 38p, streaky pork 30p; FAMILY BUTCHER, 165 Dundee St.—cheap.

## BAKERS

CRAIG, GREEN, 8 St. Peter's Buildings (Gilmore Pl.)—all night. LAWRENCE, Yeoman Pl.—best pies in Edinburgh; MURRAY, Home Baker, 139 Lauriston Pl.—average.

## GROCERS

HAY & CO., 23 Bread St; ST. CUTHBERT'S STORE, Leven Terr.. opp. Kings Theatre—good food supermarkets; HARCUS, 151 West Port—very cheap cheese and bacon, good for other groceries; COST-U-LESS—very cheap—172 Fountainbridge; KHAYYAMS, 18 Gilmore Pl.—open till 10 pm; GALBRAITH COCHRANES, 15 Tollcross, cheap.

## FISH

J. DICKSON & SON, 49 Home St.—expensive but good; P. McMILLAN, 165 Dundee St.—broken fillets 20p lb; FISHMONGER, 145 West Port—average.

## VICTUALLERS

RBT. THOMSON, 155 West Port—lentils, rice etc. also eggs—good shop, cheap.

## DELICATESSEN

CONNOISSEURS, 28 Gilmore Pl.—only delicatessen in Tollcross—mainly Polish goodies.

## BOOZE

SHERS, Fowler Terr. (off Dundee St.)—cheapest this side of Edinburgh. Open till 9 pm most nights; HENDERSONS, Tollcross—dearer. Open till 10 pm.

## SPECIALIST SHOPS

QUERNSTONE, Gilmore Pl.—multi-flavoured home-made ice cream; VEDA Health Food Shop—have their own malted bread—gourmet shop, muesli ingredients, nice yoghourt.

# LEITH WALK

## BOTTOM HALF OF LEITH WALK

### BUTCHERS

CRAIG, Crighton Pl.—good butcher late of Bread St.

### BAKERS

SNEATH, 240 Leith Walk—home baker; WOOD, 102 Duke St.

### FRUIT

JUNCTION FRUIT BAZAAR, 63 Junction St. and DRUMMONDS at no. 53 battle for cheapest fruit. PILRIG FRUIT BAZAAR, 28 Crighton Pl. (Leith Walk). Another of the chain, but not so cheap.

### GROCERS

BENSONS—cut price chain of grocers with several shops on Walk. T.McBRIDE—cut price grocer, 49 Leith Walk.

### FISH

PORT SETON FISH SUPPLY, 245 Leith Walk. Not so much cheap as good.

### VICTUALLERS AND DELICATESSEN

17 HENDERSON ST., Leith—cheap and nice.

### BOOZE

FAIRBAIRNS, Albert St. Still the cheapest booze shop in town. Open till 10 every night except Wed. and Sun; KHAYYAM, corner of Easter & Albert St. Rubayat open till 10.00 to purvey cheap booze and groceries.

## TOP HALF OF LEITH WALK

### BUTCHERS

PRATT, 65 Elm Row. Not cheap but a good butcher. DEEP FREEZE CENTRE (55 Elm Row)—frozen meat.

### BAKERS

ITALIAN, 48 Elm Row. Pizzas 12 & 15p. Rolls. Doughnuts, and chicken specialities 25p.

### FRUIT

GERHARD & DRUMMONDS in Elm Row compete for price. We prefer drummonds for quality and selection.

### GROCERS

BENSONS, corner of London Rd.

### FISH

BROWN, 55 Elm Row—OK. ROBERTS BROS., 34 Elm Row—best overall selection.

### DELICATESSENS ETC.

VALVONA & CROALLA. Elm Row—our favourite delicatessen in

town. Has its own roasted coffee from 30p lb. Wines and cheeses. Always queues but quick service and you can eat a hot pizza for 15p while you wait.

## DAIRIES
D.CUNNINGHAM, Brunswick St; MORAN, Crichton St.

## HAYMARKET/DALRY RD./GORGIE RD.

Not generally good shopping area. HAYS, 152 Gorgie Rd. is the cheapest general food store but is limited for variety. There is a small Cochrane's at either extremity of the area. For the nearest delicatessen go to Morrison St. to the Hong Kong Store, open on Sundays.

### BUTCHERS
There is a general sprinkking of butchers along the length of both streets.
PURDIE, 59 Dalry Rd: good quality.
ECONOMY FOOD PACKS, 69—71 Dalry Rd. Specialises in deep-frozen meats.
SOUNESS, 208—210 Dalry Rd. Good value.
STEVEN, 171 Gorgie Rd., cheapest mince in the area.
CITY BUTCHERS, 162 Gorgie Rd.

### FISH
Three in each road; none special. For best quality walk to Thomsons, Morrison St.

### FRUIT
Gorgie/Dalry's speciality.
GORGIE FRUIT BAZAAR, 136 Gorgie Rd. Overall cheapest in town, can be beaten sometimes. Also offers cheap eggs, boiling fowls (25p) etc. NB permanent queuing.
SALTMANS, 179 and LUMSDEN, 104 and 213. Compete bravely.
FRUITLINE, 50 Dalry Rd. Honourable mention.
SALTMANS, 63 Dalry Rd. Branch of cheap chains.
MORRISON FRUIT BAZAAR, 105 Morrison St. Another of this cheap chain.

### BAKERS
Nothing special except perhaps OVEN-FRESH BAKERY, Morrison St., open Friday nights from 11.00 pm onwards; bakehouse open rest of week after midnight; good fresh bread sold daily.

## STOCKBRIDGE/NEW TOWN

Good if scattered shopping area with concentrations of shops in Raeburn Pl., Dundas St. and Broughton St.

## BUTCHERS

GEO. CLERK, cheap and good, especially for ham; T.G. STRATH, Raeburn Pl., cheap and good speciality pies; ALEX MUNRO, 23 Broughton St.—not consistently cheap but good—Cambridge sausages and haggis.

## BAKERS

DOUGLAS, Raeburn Pl.—all night bakery, own rolls, cakes and bread; WOOD, Raeburn Pl.—branch of local chain; WHOLEFOOD CENTRE, Dundas St.—a health food shop which has Hendersons wholemeal bread and rolls every day.

## FRUIT

STEWARTS, Dundas St., known locally as Dirty Dick's, cheapest greengrocer in the area, you can tell by the queues; HENDERSONS Farm Shop, 92 Hanover St.—fresh farm grown vegetables, herbs, etc. Cheaper than you would think; SALTMAN & SON, Deanhaugh St.—cheap, almost rivals Stewarts, best in Stockbridge.

## GROCERS

FOOD FOR CASH, Broughton St; FOOD FOR CASH, 60 Dundas St; ORIENTAL GROCERIES, 49 London St.sells quite good veg. and fruit, along with general groceries. Open every day including Suns. till about 11.30—12.00; The LARDER, Raeburn St./Dean St.—general grocers, open till 10.00 including Suns. Bit of a rip-off.

## FISH

A. MUNRO, 44 Broughton St.—very good shop, especially cheap crabs, trout on Thursdays, always have good food in season, e.g. sprats; The COMMON GROUND (at Bridge, Raeburn Pl.)—every Wed. morning from a van. Get there early.

## DELICATESSENS

DELICACIES CENTRE, Barony St.—nice Polish delicatessen. Incredible Scottish Yoghourt, Polish Ham sausage, bottled fruit and cheesecake. Open Sundays (Polish an asset). EDINBURGH CHINESE CO., Dublin St.—Chinese supermarket, open Sundays, nice one!

## BOOZE

PETER DOMINIC, 30 Broughton St.—only reasonable booze shop in area. Cheap 2 litre plonk.

## SPECIALIST

DAILI MADE, Henderson Row—wholesale ice cream by the gallon, very cheap, ideal for parties; HARMONY HEALTH FOOD SHOP, Dublin St.—good bread; OLD PEOPLES WELFARE COUNCIL, off St. Stephen St.—bread and cakes, self made.

# MORNINGSIDE

Most food shops in Morningside Rd. offer fairly similar quality and value. Only a few give outstanding value. Of these, the ORCHARD (207 Morningside Rd.) is generally cheaper for fruit, cheeses, dairy food, honey, and a limited selection of meat, cooked meats, frozen food, and fish.

## BUTCHERS

GRANT SUTHERLAND, 187 Morningside Rd. sells acceptable cheap meat. He is the only butcher we've found in M'side Rd. to sell pig's trotters though most of his meat is more conventional.

## BAKERS

MURRAY Bakers, 356 Morningside Rd. Mr. Murray's bread tastes like bread—enough said; 255 MORNINGSIDE RD.—bread baked by physically handicapped.

## GROCER

COCHRANES—cheap milk and groceries.

## VICTUALLERS

CEREAL PRODUCE CO., 205 Morningside Rd.

# NEWINGTON/MARCHMONT/BRUNTSFIELD

Two exceptional delicatessens in an otherwise unexcep- area.

NEWINGTON DELICATESSEN, West Preston St. Cheapest butcher in area—mince 26p; CHARLES MacSWEEN, 130 Bruntsfield Pl., best haggis in town.

## FRUIT

MACS, 35 Marchmont Rd.—cheapest fruit in Marchmont; P. De LUCA, 25 Newington Rd.—good greengrocer, also pasta, cheese—small selection.

## GROCERS

KIBBY'S and the COOP, cheapest grocers in Marchmont. For Newington Rd./Salisbury Rd. area try COOPERS FINE FARE, salisbury.

## DELICATESSENS

ANDREW MURRAY, 188 Bruntsfield Pl.—cooked meats; The ORIENTAL GROCERS, 25 Argyle Pl. Don't miss it. Shelves crammed with Pakistani and Chinese goodies. Many different types of dried fish, home-made Indian sweetmeats and savouries (NB 'Somaca', 6p each, Indian bridies). Ethnic Chinese teas, good Indian vegetables. Open till 6.00; VICTOR HUGO Delicatessen, Melville Terr.—German-owned, modern and well stocked. Very good selection of coffee, 15 different types of pate; lots of good cheeses. Needn't be expensive. Open till 6.00.

## BOOZE

WM. THORNTON, not extortionate, i.e. 2 litres of wine, £1.50. Open till 8.00, 10.00 on Fri & Sat; HAMILTON, Lord Russell Pl: wine merchants open till 10.00.

# WHEELS AND DEALS

ITS EASIER TO STAY AT HOME

2

CIRCULAR

Edinburgh's transport problems began in the 1920's with the mushrooming of suburbia. While the housing moved out of the centre, the work, shop-ping and entertainment and other essential facilities continued to concentrate in the city centre. A pattern of city living which involved extensive travelling was established and has persisted to this day.

The inevitable problems are familiar to anyone living in the city, congestion, traffic jams, long and tedious bus journeys, dismal and inadequate suburbs and in the city the threat that commercial development will turn the centre into a concrete jungle of carparks and office blocks.

They paved paradise
And put up a parking lot
With a pink hotel, a boutique
And a swinging hot spot
Don't it always seem to go
That you don't know what
you've got
Till it's gone
They paved paradise
And put up a parking lot

Joni Mitchell

The Edinburgh Society want to tackle this problem at the roots by decentralisation and the creation of outer urban centres. The potential advantages being the relief of the centrifugal tendency of Edinburgh's traffic, the spread of traffic loads, the easing of congestion, the reduction of commuter traffic and enhanced amenities in the city centres and suburbs.

The official plan for improving Edinburgh's public transport system hangs on the Buchanan, Freeman, Fox study of transport in Edinburgh which advocates busways from the suburbs to the city centre, largely on disused railway tracks, hopefully combining speed of rail with the adaptability of the bus. However the other Buchanan proposals, already being implemented which further encourage the killer car to use the city centre, undermine hopes for these schemes.

All the Buchanan proposals are based on an estimated increase in road traffic, particularly car ownership and usage, of 110% by 1991. Professor Hendry and the Edinburgh Amenity and Transport Association have argued that the impending world fuel crisis make this figure unrealistic. For instance petrol rationing seems probable in the mid 1980's and if cars transferred to electricity the energy required for the number of cars forecast by the end of the century would need the output of 100 new 1000 Megawatt Power stations (an increase of twice the present output of the CEGB).

Hendry argues that far from a decline in the requirements for public transport over the next 20 years it is more probable that there will be a steep increase. We should therefore adopt a system which a) can deal satisfactorily and economically with the present situation; b) which has the potential for large growth and c) can be switched from one primary fuel source to another without great expense.

Hendry doubts that a bus system could cope without considerable road construction and would be difficult to adapt to different facts and so his alternative is a light railway.

The other advantages of a Light Railway would be:

1) little demand on scarce land—most already occupied by railways; 2) minimal requirement for demolition of property; 3) exploits existing assets and does not set up new and formidable barriers between areas or interfere with character of the city; 4) less environmental disturbance; 5)(a) no air pollution; (b) visually unobtrusive; 6) Construction can begin without usual delays while property acquired or cleared; 7) would help free streets for remaining traffic and minimise need for new roads; 8) provision of reliable

rapid and frequent city transport will make restrictions on cars more acceptable; 9) safe.

It is estimated that the full system would cost £20 million and could take 7 years to complete. Many other European cities are at present extending or redeveloping their metros; Hendry suggests Edinburgh adopt a system similar to those proposed for Frankfurt or the Tyneside, with light railcars with a carrying capacity of 170 (60 seats) and a top speed of 50 m.p.h.

Attractive as it seems the Light Railway seems unlikely to gain official approval and meanwhile we've got to cope with traffic as best we can.

Without the Railway buses are the only public transport in Edinburgh. The numbers of passenger journeys on Corporation buses peaked in 1950 at 286 million journeys. At that time only 5% of journeys to work were made by private car or motorcycle yet 50% of the road traffic was caused by private vehicles. Since then bus traffic has fallen by approximately 4% per annum to 221 million in 1960 and 154 million in 1970. While increases in fares (minimum fare in 1960 3d, 1970 3p, more increases imminent) may account for some of the loss the critical factor has been the switch to private transport. Congestion is the buses' worst enemy. The overall average speed in Edinburgh is 9.8 miles/hour (exactly the same as cable cars in 1914—18); during peak hours this drops to an abysmal 2—4 miles/hour. Average speed is dropping, having been 11.3 in 1969 and one-man buses have further slowed services.

One-man buses are not all bad; while individual services are slower, they have helped overcome the chronic staff shortage and increase the number of buses on each route.

The Transport Dept. are already investigating other ways of improving the system, particularly alternative means of fare collection, but such improvements only plug the gaps and are not an answer to the atrophying of public transport. As long as we retain the 19th century view that public transport must pay for itself we will have the vicious circle of raising fares in the face of falling passenger levels with the consequent high fares forcing more people off the system, increasing road congestion, lowering bus efficiency, raising fares etc.

What are needed are more radical restrictions on private cars in the city centre combined with positive incentives to make public transport more attractive. Any combination of bus lanes, bus only streets, pedestrian areas, subsidised fares, free buses would be a help, but time is running out. The corporation should get off its arse and try something.

The longer they take, the more likely we are to choke on the crud from the infernal combustion engine.

Meanwhile, here are the services that exist at present and how to use them.

For comprehensive information on services, prices, season tickets etc contact Edinburgh Corporation Transport Dept., 14 Queen St. (225 3941) or the Transport Information Kiosk, Waverley Bridge. For passenger enquiries phone 556 5656. Current fares are: minimum 3p for 1 to 3 stages, children's flat fare, dog fare, shoppabus fare; elderly persons' fare; 6p for 4—6 stages, 9p maximum fare; 12p flat fare for all night service buses.

Making use of Edinburgh bus services for stranger or native can be simplified by realising that all Corporation bus routes (with two exceptions) have stops within 50 yards of Princes St.

A good plan for the complete stranger is to make for Princes St. and the Transport Info Kiosk on Waverley Bridge. A good alternative is the excellent Edinburgh Corporation Bus Map at every covered bus shelter which with the help of a local can soon get you around (the map is available at Waverley Bridge and at 5p is a best buy for tourist or resident).

The main bus stops around Princes St. are

Waverley—top of Waverley steps—buses 2/12, 3, 4, 9, 10, 11, 15, 16, 24/29, 26, 28, 31/33, 44.

Tron (High St.)—buses 1, 34/35, 45.

North Bridge (beside Waverley)—5, 7/37, 8, 14, 34/35, 49.

West End (of Princes St.)—2/12, 3, 4, 9, 10, 11, 13, 15, 16, 17/47, 18/41, 19, 20, 22, 24/29, 26/28, 31/33, 34/35, 44.

Mound (Princes St.)—23, 27, 41, 42.

Waverley Bridge—30, 43.

St. Andrew Sq.—17/47, 19, 20, 22, 42.

The only bus routes which do not come close to Princes St. are nos. 32 and 36.

REMEMBER if you've no money, it's legal to travel by bus by giving your address to the conductor/driver.

First buses on most routes start around 05.00. Last buses from Princes St. approx. 23.30. Thereafter Night Buses.

COMPLAINTS: Any complaints to R.E. Bottrill, Transport Manager, Edinburgh Corporation Transport Dept., 14 Queen St., Edinburgh

LOST PROPERTY: Also at 14 Queen St. Allow 24 hours to reach Lost Property Dept. unless valuable when efforts will be made to trace bus. Lost Property Sales are advertised in Evening News, usually last Friday in month. Sales at Aitkens' Auctioneers, Broughton St., first Tuesday in month. Property sold 3 months after found.

PRIVATE HIRE: The corporation run a private hire dept. from their HQ in Queen St. The pricing system is complicated and based on mileage.

BUYING OLD BUSES: For info write to Queen St. and ask to be put on their mailing list of prospective buyers. You'll then receive information on any forthcoming sales. You can pick up an old bus for as little as £125—200.

WALKING: If you're lucky enough to find a pad in the central area walking can be a viable alternative to the clogged transport network. Suitable areas might be Newington, Marchmont, Tollcross, Haymarket, New Town, High St. From these, most central areas can be walked within 20 minutes.

BIKES: If you want to buy bikes the best way is by going to the police sales of lost property at J. Aitkens, Broughton St. Sales are held on Tuesdays and to check if one is on see Friday's 'Evening News'. Also worth checking out for second-hand bikes are Bike Shop, Kings Rd., Portobello and Hyde's, 38 St. Leonard St.

CARS: Last year in Edinburgh 52 people were sacrificed to the killer car. 2330 people were injured. Every week 45 people are hospitalised for a month or more directly from car accidents.

That's not all, the internal combustion engine is inefficient. Those grey unburned hydro carbons that pour out of the exhaust are wasted energy and they are choking us. Pollutants include carbon monoxide, sulphur dioxide, lead compounds, nitrogen oxides, vanadium, cadmium smoke and noise. California already has laws on crud emission which would put every car in Britain off the roads, yet we never learn, e.g. cars consume 40% of the world's lead production as a petrol additive, one third of this is emitted in car exhausts—lead poisoning can cause death. A car uses more oxygen in 600 miles (say Edinburgh to Lands End) than one person in a life time, etc. If you're still interested after all that, here's info on buying, running and hiring in Edinburgh.

BUYING: Buy abroad. Schipol Airport, Amsterdam is good or alternatively, ex factory. You have to pay import tax but still save £100+. Similarly buying in Britain for export within a year saves you purchase tax in this country. The Customs House, Commercial St., Leith (554 2421) has the info.

BUYING NEW IN BRITAIN: It is possible to get around 12% discount especially for cash by shopping around and saying last place offered 10%.

BUYING SECOND-HAND: Best bet if you have cash and a discriminating eye or tame mechanic is the Ingliston Car Auctions run by Auto Auctions (Scotland), 334 3209. Every Thursday 12.00–18.00. Over 250 every week. Beware of resprays, painted tyres, etc. Best tactics—go along for a few weeks just to learn the ropes. Buy the price list (available at auction) showing actual price of all cars over £50 sold in the previous month. When bidding set yourself a target price and don't exceed it—if car does not live up to description return it within 24 hours. Be firm, they'll take it back. Regulations of sale on display at auction—read them.

If no cash try to avoid H.P., even a bank overdraft is cheaper. Evening News probably best local guide to used cars but prices £100+, more expensive than auctions.

RUNNING A CAR: Back in 1969 'Which' estimated that it cost 2p a mile to run a mini 12,000 miles a year even doing your own repairs. The latest AA estimation is a staggering £560/annum to run a 'family' car. So here's some help to keep costs to a minimum.

Insurance: Brokers are the best deal. We recommend Manor, 12 Manor Pl. (225 7595), Midlothian, 26 York Pl. (556 1100), NUS (esp. for students), 12 Dublin St. (556 5678), Coates, 22 Manor Pl. (556 9711, 225 1828.)

Cheap Repairs: Coachbuilding, resprays etc.—I.D. Developments, Unit 4, Whitehill Industrial Estate, Bathgate (51-52086); Chris McGuigan, Abbeyhill Railway Arches (667 4968), George Packwood, Leith Walk Goods Yard (554 6167), Donald Scott, Motor Cycle Yard, Buccleuch St. (nr. Meadow Bar).

Cheap spares: Scrap yards can supply all your needs. Hassle over price. Try Auto Parts, Gogarbank (334 2010), Auto Spares, 2 Gogarbank (334 1892), Edinburgh Motor Spares & Salvage, Ramsay Colliery, Loanhead, Sports Car Breakers, Claylands Farm, Newbridge (Ratho 498).

**Cheap Petrol Stations:** petrol's all the same so buy the cheapest. Jet Causewayside Service Station, Claymore, Portobello High St., Croall & Croall, Glenogle Rd., Leamington Terr., Roseburn, SMT Service Station, Roseburn St., Willowbrae Service Station, Willowbrae Rd., Maybury Roundabout, Texaco, Asda Supermarket, Milton Rd. West, Golden, Portobello and Currie, VIP, East Preston St., Mobil, Glasgow Rd., Corstorphine, Fina, Saughton Road North.

**Motor Cycle Dealers:** E. Taskers, Broughton St. Probably best in town. They carry a lot of small spares for most m/cycles, usually very helpful, also know bikes inside out. West Pier Motor Cycles, Brandon Terr. Triumph and BSA agents. They do repairs, but spares poor. Edgar Bros, Leith Walk. Agents for Honda and Yamaha. Carry a fair amount of spares for new bikes. Chathams, Abbeyhill. Pretty much the same. EUMCC, next to Meadow Bar. Has a fair amount of secondhand spares, a good pool of knowledge and will help. Boris and Steve, 26 Lauriston Pl. (229 4561).

CAR HIRE: Of the 11 car hire firms in Edinburgh the cheapest we found were West Savile Motors (667 5273) and Wards Car Rentals (556 3126). SMT are more expensive but give a good service. Hire is normally restricted to over 21, over 1 year driving experience. Carnies, 552 5521.

One nice alternative to petrol driven cars may be Calor Gas (Butane or Propane and Natural Gas—Methane). Harold Bates, a farmer in Devon pioneered kits using chicken shit as a source of methane to power his car. The Calor Gas Co. and L.P.G. also market conversion kits which cost around £120, including fitting.

These kits have the advantage that they burn to carbon dioxide and water only and do not contain lead tetraethyl or other toxic anti-knock additives, they can be used in high compression engines (up to 16:1 compression)

97

without causing pre-ignition and are untaxed and as such cost about half the price of petrol per mile.

Against their use are—the cost of conversion, the fitting of a bulky gas cylinder and the fact that if popular the government would slap tax on these fuels.

If anyone is interested in helping to produce a conversion kit please phone STEWART—552 3960. Another useful address is Harold Bates, Penny Rowden, Totnes, Devon.

**USEFUL ADDRESSES**

EDINBURGH SOCIETY—S. Mathew, 14 Lynedoch Pl., Edinburgh

EDINBURGH AMENITY & TRANSPORT ASSOCIATION, 47 Northumberland St., Edinburgh

Prof. S.W. Hendry, Dept. of Civil Engineering and Building Science, University of Edinburgh.

# HOUSING

Edinburgh Housing is characterised by isolated communities whose main connection with the heart of the city and all its facilities is an overloaded bus system which is likely to be getting worse not better. The forces of development, throw more and more people into the outer suburbs, which do not have the amenities these communities need to have a degree of independence from the centre. The city centre, jealously attempting to retain its importance as a cultural and consumer focal point, despite the ravages of the developers and the University, has managed to turn its former residents into full time tourists.

Whilst trying to convey the problems and possibilities of finding a home in Edinburgh, the first question is,—do you really want to live in the urban environment.

### Country Pads

If you're tired of coping with the city, life is mellower and cheaper in the country. The immediate outskirts are expensive and continually threatened by sprawling suburbia, but travel further out and it's fairly free from commuters. For information on ready-made empty houses and cottages try the relevant county council (Berwickshire for one keeps a list of empty property, sent on request.

The National Trust, Forestry Commission, British Rail, The Crofters Commission and the National Coal Board all occasionally have property and land for sale or rent, but even this can be out of the average communes price range. Look around and where you find empty houses check up, although there might be a variety of ressons for the vacancy. If a building is due for demolition by property developers, a little historical research might help you get a preservation order, which would frustrate the developers and give you a chance.

Land and farms are generally expensive. Before buying the land have it surveyed and determine what planning restrictions there might be. Even the contract itself is better left to lawyers who will handle the contracts and the conveyance. Often if the land does not already have buildings upon it, planning permission may be difficult and expensive to obtain. For the more adventurous or commune-minded, old village schools or abandoned churches are good raw materials—write to the appropriate county council education department or to the Church of Scotland, 121 George Street, Both are much cheaper than houses and the government offers grants of 50%-75% of conversion costs—which means you have a fun home for peanuts and sweat. Generally the further from Edinburgh the cheaper the place. Going price till recently was £1000 for a naked Church.

What you do with the inside of any buildings on the land and even exterior decoration do not require planning approval, but permanent extensions of one tenth or 1750 cu.ft. on the building do require permission. You may get a visit from the local Health Officer, and the Local Authority has power to prosecute, so be sure that sanitation and refuse in particular are adequately dealt with. The mobile home and structures not built into the ground do not need permission but this does render you vulnerable to being moved around every 28 days or so. Tents, domes, or any other unfixed structure could be a hassle unless you like changes of scenery.

## Mobile Homes

If you have a phobia against solid walls, or roofs, get a mobile-van. Unless you have an HGV Licence, 20-35 cwt. should be adequate; your best finds being from Government Surplus (GPO or Corporation) or any large firm that is re-equipping. What you do with the van is limited only by your imagination. If you decide to instal windows in a van less than five years old, in order to avoid purchase tax as a private vehicle, you should complete the conversion to a "motor caravan" with sleeping, washing, and eating facilities.

## Building Your Own

For anyone interested in constructing their home be it domes, log cabins, utopias or cardboard mansions the best source-books are the **Whole Earth Catalogue**—(Penguin)-mainly American information and **The Survival Scrapbook 1. Shelter**. (Unicorn Bookshop, Brighton) both of which you can peruse or buy in Better Books, Forrest Road. Another useful address is The British Commune Movement (Richard Secombe, 2 Chapel Hill Ashestt, and Bridgewater, Somerset) will provide a useful form of contacts and ideas.

## Flats

If you don't think you've got it together to face the Lothians frontier life, or you can't face the hassles of being too far away from the city where its all happening (see rest of book), you can still establish a way of living that can appeal to the communal instinct. That marvellous device of Scots architecture, the "stairs" has great potential as the focal point of a whole tenement, with different levels being used communally. For most people, however, Edinburgh presents enough problems just finding a place to stay.

FURNISHED FLATS: 3 or 4-bedroomed flats should never be more than £10-£15 weekly (depending on facilities, NOT the number of occupants). Small or no deposit. Usually pay in advance. Look for a bedroom per person; sitting/dining room, kitchen bathroom/w.c.; furnishings including everything from bed clothes to cutlery; heating in every room and lighting inclusive in rent. Don't sign a lease or agreement on restriction on behaviour.

UNFURNISHED FLATS: Cheaper, usually by half, than furnished, but scarce. Extra costs will be rates, fixtures and fittings. Landlords will probably expect rent quarterly in advance and may require references.

BEDSITS: Singles cost £3-£5 weekly, doubles about £3 per person. Sharing cooking facilities (otherwise expect a miniature cooker,) bath and lavatory. Fairly free of restrictions in practice, but avoid sharing the same building as the landlord. Heating through slot meter usually.

DIGS: Average charges, part board and lodgings, are £6.50-£7.50, slightly less for sharing. Heating and laundry usually extra, but all bedding is provided. Most digs are outside the central area, so take account of busfares. Look for a friendly landlady and minimal restrictions on noise, visitors, etc.

## Where Advertised

DAILY PAPERS: The Scotsman is good for flat buyers but not cheap rented accommodation. The Evening News advertises furnished flats, digs and bedsits and hits the streets about 14.30. Phone as soon as the ad appears.

POSTCARD BOARDS: A few of the smaller newsagents provide this service for a small fee—keep your eyes open. Otherwise try student unions—free noticeboards are usually provided here. Try the Student Centre at Bristo Street first, then Grindley Street, Teviot Place and Chamber Street Unions.

## Accommodation Agencies

Their usual technique is to advertise the flat but not the address—for that you go inside. Once there, don't sign any written agreement—these are unnecessary and only give an advantage to the agency. An accommodation or estate agent is not allowed to demand or accept money just for registering your name or supplying a list of homes to let. However, if the agency really provides other services, like inspecting the flat or arranging for you to visit it, then they are legally entitled to demand a fee. Once you've accepted a flat or house, query any agency fee before paying it. If the explanation of the services supposedly provided is unsatisfactory, refuse to pay the fee and seek legal advice.

## Rent Tribunal

If you're renting a furnished flat and have grounds to feel you're paying too much, go to the Rent Tribunal, 6 Coates Place (225 1200 Ext. 213) for a rent reduction. Once the Tribunal has fixed a rent the landlord cannot lawfully ask for more.

The tenant applying to have his rent fixed will be asked to fill in a form and be given help to do so from one of the Tribunal's staff. The Tribunal then asks the landlord about the accommodation—the tenant can check this information and should contest any inaccurate items. Usually the Tribunal will then inspect the property and fix a hearing at which both sides may employ a lawyer but legal aid is not available. The local council can prosecute or the tenant can take court action if the landlord charges more after the rent if fixed.

One disadvantage of applying to the Rent Tribunal is that the landlord may retaliate by trying to evict the tenant. But the tenant with a written fixed-term agreement is entitled to stay until that expires, providing he keeps to its terms. The tenant with no agreement, or one which doesn't specify a period, is automatically given up to six months' security on application for rent reduction.

Finally, if you're moving into furnished accommodation, check the register kept by the Rent Tribunal to make sure you're not being overcharged.

### Corporation Housing

There has been a considerable change in the housing situation over the last year. Since the relaxation of the qualifications for Corporation housing the number of unlet houses in "surplus areas" (like Pilton and Niddrie) has fallen from 700 to about 160, but the waiting list has escalated from 6000 to over 8000. Any normal householder can now qualify for a council house, but the uptake of these houses is more an indication of the pressure on housing in general than the product of any startling improvement in conditions. Most of the 8000 remaining are holding out for vacancies on better estates (since the chances of transfer later to another estate are negligible); but there may well be no surplus houses in a year's time.

If you want to see about a Corporation house, and this now includes men and women who haven't legalised their separation, write to the Director of Housing, House Letting Department, Anchor Close.

## Homelessness

For too many, however, there is the unease and humiliation of homelessness. The National Assurance Act of 1948 places the onus on local authorities to provide homes for those who have 'unexpectedly' been rendered homeless, but the conditions of housing were left vague and Edinburgh Corporation has been allowed to house families in buildings that should have been condemned long ago.

The first step for a homeless family is often forced 'separation', the father being left to fend for himself, crashing at a friend's place or paying for a bed in one of the squalid Grassmarket hostels, while the mother and kids are moved to a boarding house paid by the Corporation. For the lucky few there are 20 Corporation 'scattered houses' where rents are heavily subsidised but length of stay is temporary. Unfortunately, a stay in one of the Corporation's emergency 'flats' at Duddingston (for 4 families) but no fathers allowed except between 18.00 and 22.00 hours), or Johnstone Terrace (for 24 families) is more likely. An indication of the standard of these places is the fact that the Castle Garrison moved its married quarters from the Johnstone Terrace flats in 1963 because the place was considered unfit for human habitation then.

The Corporation has been the largest single agent of evictions (mainly for rent arrears) in the city. Much of the blame for rent arrears lay in the system of fortnightly payments to a central office some distance away. Local Rent Collectors greatly improved the situation in Pilton, so if you have no collector, agitate at your rent office.

If it does reach the stage of 6 months arrears, after a cycle of letters and warnings you will be faced with eviction. Leaving before the sherriff arrives could be misconstrued by the authorities as "voluntary termination", which would delay your reconsideration by another 6 months even after repayment of arrears. Don't move out of the city (you have to be resident for one month before the application) and if all your rent has been paid you can begin again, only with rather less choice than before.

## Eviction and Notice to Quit

No tenant can be evicted without a court order, however

badly he has behaved and in most cases the landlord must take preliminary steps before he can apply to the Sheriff Court. The usual way of trying to get a tenant to leave is to serve him with a legal document called a 'notice to quit', which must be in writing and should be checked for validity with a solicitor. It must give the tenant a minimum of four week's notice ending on a day when the rent is due to be paid.

However, the landlord cannot force the tenant to leave without going to the second stage—applying for an eviction order. When this application is made there will be a court hearing, where the tenant has an opportunity to put his case. If the tenant has a lease or agreement which has run out the landlord still needs to serve a notice to quit.

In the case of furnished tenancies a court order will be given almost automatically if no appearance is entered by the defendant stating intention to lodge defences, but the court can prevent an eviction order becoming operative for up to 28 days.

For most unfurnished tenancies the court must be satisfied that eviction is reasonable on legal grounds. A tenant who has paid his rent and kept the terms of his tenancy can be evicted only if his landlord (or his close relatives) has greater need of the property.

If a landlord or any person tries to evict a tenant without a court order he is guilty of a criminal offence. Even if he does not resort of eviction by physical means the landlord might still be found guilty of harassment.

At all times remember to seek legal advice quickly (legal aid is available in respect of court proceedings). Your local councillor might also help.

### Useful addresses

Citizens Advice Bureau, 58 Dundas Street, a friendly and potentially useful source of information. (556 6179).

Rent Registration Service, 6 Coates Crescent, to help sort out your legal problems with renting. (225 5534).

Shelter Housing Aid Centre, 8 Frederick Street (225 6058), have a lot of experience in handling homeless, or the potentially homeless.

# GRASS ROOTS

Grass Roots activism is a growing force in Edinburgh politics. There are literally dozens of such groups in the city, most of which have been formed in the last few years. Few councillors can now afford not to court the support of their local association. While activism often waxes and wanes with issues, the ground support of the 'silent majority' (sic) is strong and increasingly associations are organising on a more continuous basis.

One way to do this is by continuously generating new projects, to maintain interest. For example the Linksview Association was formed to fight a rates complaint but spread to a campaign to improve the amenities of the area, the setting up of an adventure playground, a playschool etc. Similarly the Pilton association are very active with summer playscheme projects, community councillor candidates, community newspaper and video projects.

Other associations have generated their support by taking on one all encompassing project which can be the focal point for their activities. The Leith Festival, Craigmillar Festival and proposed Sighthill Gala fall into this type. Below is a cameo history of the most advanced of these—the CRAIG-MILLAR FESTIVAL SOCIETY, to show what can be achieved.

## CRAIGMILLAR: THE START OF AN ALTERNATIVE

Craigmillar, for long tucked away beyond Arthur's Seat to the South West and forgotten by the rest of the city, has been increasingly impressing itself on the city's consciousness as a place where "something is happening".

Over the years there has been a succession of organisations which have given militant voice to local concerns: The Tennant's Defense League in the Thirties; the Victory Council of the War Years, the Joint Council of the 'miners' union and others. The Joint Council disintegrated in the early sixties and was succeeded by the Craigmillar Festival.

The Festival has two roots—the old galas typical of much of Scotland and the Royal Pageants enacted by the Scottish nobility in 1906 & 1927.

The interesting thing to note is that the conjunction of the gala tradition and the tradition of struggle against deprivation are, in the Festival Society, mutually supporting. Social activities, such as a Festival, require facilities other than housing units. The Planning Workshop attacks the poverty of the existing provision of the local environment which severely limits the possibilities of community life. The recent Planning Workshop Conference showed its concern, dealing with all aspects of Craigmillar as a whole—transport, road safety, education, health, physical and mental, social welfare, the economic conditions, as well as the more obvious problems of housing deterioration and the lack of facilities.

Starting with nothing but a handful of schoolkids and lots of enthusiasm, the first festival was a success. The festival struggled on a shoestring. Its next break was to have any losses up to £100 underwritten.

1968 saw a flare up in the community centre saga when 'the freeze' saw it cut from the city budget. A concerted campaign of demonstrations, press support and council lobbying only gained assurances that it would be given top priority in the future. Five years later, 1973, work on the site is scheduled to begin.

In late '69 the Festival Society submitted several radical proposals to the Scottish Office's Urban Aid Project scheme. These proposals basically concerned financial support to allow the community to develop and explore its own potential.

The proposals were accepted and the initial results have been recorded in The Report of the Craigmillar Festival Society, 1970-71 entitled 'A Community On the Move' by Helen Crummy.

The Urban Aid programme was given a further boost this year when the Council gave the go-ahead to the Lord Provost's Committee's Pilot Scheme for Craigmillar. A budget of £20,000 covering extra staff, Transport, Administration and a community project fund of £5,000 has already enabled a number of projects to get off the ground. Other activities include pre-school playgroups run by local mothers, summer play-schemes, and an Arts Workshop which they hope to expand in the coming years, while the Planning Workshop has been actively involved in the redevelopment plans for Newcraighall village and the Craigmillar Castle Housing Renovation scheme.

The Craigmillar Festival News is also brought out periodically by the Society and is distributed free to 8,000 houses in the ward, keeping residents in touch with local developments.

Impressive as its record is to date, the Festival Society still has a long way to go in getting to grips with the roots of their disposed heritage and transforming Craigmillar into a sympathetic human environment. But the future, as most people recognise, lies with that "40% aged 20 or under", the youth of Craigmillar.

## OTHER GROUPS

To find out what other groups are involved in greater detail contact your local association or the Edinburgh Tenants Coordinating Committee.

In addition to the Tenants Association, there are many active Amenity groups, which tend to be more middle class organisations, more interested in preservation of existing amenity than in deprived areas. The Cockburn Association coordinates 32 of these groups and is trying genuinely to escape from its preoccupation with the 'New Town'.

## USEFUL ADDRESSES

EDINBURGH TENANTS COORDINATING COMMITTEE, Chairman Jim Smith, 31/4 West Granton Loan, Edin. 4 (552 7582). For up to date info on all Edinburgh's Tenants Associations.

COCKBURN ASSOCIATION, 10 Albyn Pl., Edin. 2 (225 5085): 98 years young, rather establishment, but still the most effective of Edinburgh's Amenity societies. Coordinates 32 other Amenity Groups across the city. Recent successful campaigns include the defeat of plans for a 260 ft. skyscraper at Haymarket.

EDINBURGH COUNCIL OF SOCIAL SERVICE, Ainslie House, 11 St. Colme St., Edin. 3 (225 4604). The council's traditional family casework is being adapted to combine with community development activities so as to meet needs of individuals and groups, especially by encouraging them to help themselves.

HOUSING ACTION CENTRE, 9 Mariscat Rd., Glasgow: grass roots information, research etc. on housing and community action in Scotland. Lots of contacts.

CRAIGMILLAR SOCIETY, secretary Mrs. Helen Crummy, 108 Montcastle Drive South, Edin. 15 (669 7344). Enough said!

LEITH FESTIVAL COMMITTEE, secretary John Masson, Leith Community Centre, Newkirkgate, Leith (554 4750)—the Other Community Festival.

LINKSVIEW AND TOLBOOTH WYND TENANTS ASSOCIATION, Amelia Whiteford, 31/6 Linksview House, Tolbooth Wynd, Edin. (554 5955).Started to fight a rates hassle extended into other projects including an Adventure Playground.

TOLLCROSS RESIDENTS ASSOCIATION, Mrs. G. Suttie, 4 Drumdryan St., Edin. 3 (229 4919).

WESTER HAILES ASSOCIATION OF TENANTS, 4/51 Hailesland Park, Edinburgh.

SOUTH SIDE ASSOCIATION, J. D. MacMillan, 18 George Sq., (667 1011 day, 556 7100 night) exists to protect interests of those living or working in Cowgate, Causewayside, Holyrood Park to Meadows and Lauriston area.

GORGIE/DALRY PARENTS & COMMUNITY ACTION GROUP, Mrs. Anderson, 10 West End Pl., Edin. 11 (337 1076).

GRASSMARKET ASSOCIATION, Fiona Masson, 86 West Bow.

LOCHEND TENANTS ASSOCIATION, Mrs. Watson, 10/6 Lochend House.

PILRIG ASSOCIATION, W. G. Gurkel, 2 Cambridge Gdns.

PILTON TENANTS ASSOCIATION, Tony Graham, 31 West Granton Terr. (552 6799).

CASTLE ROCK SCHEME, 26 York Pl.—housing association.

STREET RESEARCH BULLETIN, 86 Railton Rd., London S.E.24. Acts as a clearing house for research and organising, education and communication on community action.

EDINBURGH POVERTY ACTION GROUP, Citizens Rights Office, 11 Castle St., Edin. 2 (226 6349). Graham Exton; pressure group, really into community action. Work mainly through projects, nurseries, slum landlords, employment agency, etc,

## EDINBURGH WOMEN'S LIBERATION GROUP

The Women's Liberation Movement is now three years old in Britain. Do we still need to explain why women need liberated? We probably do, since "Women's lib." has become the target for cheap jokes, and suffers from a great deal of uninformed criticism.

The modern Liberation Movement differs from most earlier feminist movements in the breadth of issues with which it deals. The long term aim is different too—not simply want equality with men as men are at present and while society as a whole remains unchanged. On the contrary they want to see a society in which both men and women are able to live freer lives, no longer trapped by sex stereotypes.

Although men have a lot to gain too, a separate WOMEN'S movement is necessary. This is something, we know, which seems a bit contradictory to outsiders. Firstly it remains the case that men do gain substantial benefits from the present system—in material terms in higher wages, more skilled work, having a meal ready when they get home etc. etc. and also in less tangible psychological and social terms. Men will cling to these advantages, while women have nothing to lose but their kitchen sinks.

## SORE POINTS 3

"This your friendly DJ Jimmy speaking"

to Mrs. John Smith:

"Now tell our listeners all about yourself...
What does your husband do?"

C.L.C.

A women's-only movement is needed to help women understand (through discussion with other women) the shared and social nature of their problems, to gain experience and confidence in organising a movement, speaking in public and so on. In addition womens lib. are rediscovering women's place in history, important for any group whose achievements have been ignored or denied.

If you feel that the subjection of women is part of a more general oppression under capitalism that you'll find great scope for women's lib within most left wing groups—see "Politics".

Nationally the WL movement has held several large conferences, the latest was attended by over 800 women. Recent national campaigns which many local groups have been involved in have been the campaign to keep the payment of family allowances to women, and the fight for an anti-discrimination bill.

In the last 3 years most local campaigns have centred around 4 themes, which were adopted by the movement as 4 minimum demands. These were:

Equal pay, Equal job and educational opportunities, Free contraception and abortion on demand, Free child-care facilities, available at any time over the 24 hour period.

In Edinburgh Women's Lib are presently involved in a nursery campaign and held a public meeting in the

Churchill Theatre. From that meeting a pressure group was set up. They have prepared a Report on their ideas on nurseries and child-care, for submission to a joint working party of the Corporation Education and Social Work departments.

Women's Lib are also hoping to set up a "Women's House" in Edinburgh, which could become a centre of refuge for battered wives and other women requiring immediate accommodation and help—practical and emotional.

They have set up study groups on various topics—these include equal pay, children's literature and marriage. Members are free to attend any of these they wish.

After the last Scottish Women's Liberation Conference, a Scottish Workshop was established in Edinburgh. This serves as a co-ordinating centre for all the Scottish groups, an office, a book centre (books and pamphlets can be read there and there is also a large stock of books for sale), and a meeting place.

The address of the Workshop is 31 Royal Terrace. Telephone 031-556 5655. Groups meet every Monday and Wednesday evening at the Workshop at 7.45 p.m.

# GAY EDINBURGH

Numerically, the number of homosexuals in Edinburgh is 20,000: but the strength of the city's gay community is assessed by the number of homosexuals who are prepared to stand up and be identified as such. The past twelve months has been a great upsurge of activity.

The largest homosexual organisation in Edinburgh is the Scottish Minorities Group. Its Edinburgh Branch has about 100 members and is probably the most active in Scotland. The main activity at the moment is the fight for sexual law reform. SMG is promoting a Parliamentary Bill based on the English 1967 Sexual Offences Act, but incorporating many improvements on that far-from-perfect piece of legislation. Almost anticipating part of the proposed reform, the Lord Advocate, Norman Wylie (Cons Edinburgh Pentlands), issued a departmental letter stating that there will be no prosecutions in Scotland for sex between consenting adults in private, and assuring homosexuals of complete police support in the extent of blackmail or robbery.

The roots of discrimination and repression run deep in our society, particularly family socialism and capitalist culture. Reform and Education, while necessary, cannot be a permanent solution while existing social structures remain.

Edinburgh University officially held a Teach-In on Homosexuality in the George Square Theatre during March 1973. "A major historical event" enthused "**Scottish International**" in their report of the proceedings. Certainly no-one was left in any doubt about the progress made in Edinburgh in recent months.

But there are other places which provide regular opportunity to socialise. The gay pubs in Edinburgh are The Kenilworth (Rose Street), the Downstairs Bar of the Abercromby Hotel (Abercromby Place) and the Underworld, a pub on the corner of Northumberland Street at Dundas Street. Nowhere is the clientele 100% homosexual however. The regular Gay Disco run by SMG on Saturdays at 23 George Square, ceased at the end of June. The place became too small and new and larger premises are hoped for sometime in 1974. Calton Hill and the lavatory beside Woolworths are sexual pick-up points. Do so AT YOUR OWN RISK.

**The EDINBURGH UNIVERSITY GAY GROUP a newly founded Students' Group which is open to students at other colleges. Has its own room at Societies Centre, Hill Place (opposite Nicholson Sq.). President: Roderick Hall, Secretary: Steve Black.**

**GAY LIBERATION FRONT, c/o Blyth, top flat right, 141 Dundee Street, Edinburgh, 11.**

**MINORITY RIGHTS GROUP, 36 Cravan Street, London WC 2. Supports all groups suffering discrimination.**

The national newspaper is "**Gay News**" (price 15p) obtainable at better bookshops and newsagents, otherwise direct from G.N. 34d Redcliffe Square, London SW 10. (6 month subscription £1.90). Scottish Correspondent is Ian Dunn (031-667 7473). Press Officer and National Secretary of Scottish Minorities Group is John Breslin, 214 Clyde Street, Glasgow, G1 4JZ, to whom all enquiries about SMG should be referred.

## POLITICS

### STRAIGHT EDINBURGH

Edinburgh is a middle-class city and this is mirrored in its local political life. The Labour party has gained ascendancy only with the last year, replacing Conservatism with conservatism.

Too much can be made of Edinburgh's particular class composition, however. The problems of Edinburgh, like any other local authority, spring from a distribution of power and physical resources which is totally outside the control of local politicians and mandarins. And in this lies the essential gulf between conventional politics and alternative politics. The primary fact of our social experience is our lack of control over the nature of our society. The general characteristics of our society are created by blind economic forces and bolstered by a conception of life, an ideology, which justifies this state of affairs. The only control over our lives, in general terms, is a bureaucratic control, which is undemocratic, oppressive and restrictive. The alternative is to replace this double oppression with a society in which human consciousness and human needs are paramount. The issue before us is popular power — over work, schools, media, everything.

There are, naturally, differences about how this is to be achieved (see above) but alternative politics is about changing the world.

People who want to change the world don't usually become Town Councillors. Their political motivation ranges from misguided idealism (rare) to careerism, desire for prestige or the furtherance of business interests. If that's your scene, it's not hard — there's plenty of room at the top. Although membership figures for the conventional parties (Labour, Liberal, Scot. Nats and Conservatives, the Progressives having collapsed as a serious (sic) party) are high, the level of activism is very low. The most active group, the Labour Party, have probably about 200 activists, or half a dozen per ward on average.

Under local government reorganisation, Edinburgh becomes a district authority under South East Region. As District authority it "retains responsibility for" housing and local planning within the context of the regional 'strategic plan'. The regional authority has overall control of education, social services and most of the important functions. The reorganisation is essentially a bureaucratic rationalisation, bringing power no nearer to or remote from the people. e.g. house-building will still be held back by crippling interest rates (60% of Edinburgh's annual Housing Revenue Account goes to pay back interest), rents will be pushed up by Tory Housing Finance Acts; primary and secondary education (whether comprehensive or not) will still be retarded by grossly inadequate resources and bureaucratic control of educational policy.

There are the promised community councils, of course, which may have a very worthwhile consciousness-raising function, but which under reorganisation plans are to have neither formal political power or financial support.

It's a depressing scene, but no more depressing than any other of Britain's cities. Straight Edinburgh is straight Glasgow with a Barnton accent.

## MPS AND COUNCILLORS

The following list of M.P.s was correct in May 1973. In most cases the address given is the home, not the business address. To find the names and addresses of your local councillors go to the city chambers or phone them at 225 2424.

## MEMBERS OF PARLIAMENT:

EDIN SOUTH: Michael Clark Hutchison (Con.),16 Maunsel St., London, SW1, Tel: 01-828 1108. Edin. Office: 19 Newington Rd., Edinburgh, 9. Tel: 667 5783.

EDIN NORTH: The Earl of Dalkeith (Con), Eildon Hall, Melrose, Tel: 083 52-2705.

EDIN LEITH: Ronald King Murray (Lab.),38 Primrose Bank Rd., Edinburgh, 5. Tel:552 5602. Chambers: 30 Great King St., Edinburgh, 3. Tel: 552 5602.

EDIN CENTRAL: Tom Oswald (Lab), 28 Seaview Terr.,Edinburgh 15. Tel: 669 5569.

EDIN WEST: J.A. Stodart (Con), Lorimers, North Berwick. Tel: 0620-2457;

EDIN EAST: Gavin Strang (Lab), 22 Southfield Pl., Edinburgh, 15. Tel: 669 5999.

EDIN PENTLANDS: Norman Wylie (Con), 30 Lauder Rd., Edinburgh, 9. Tel: 667 8377.

## MOBILISING

Successful pressure group activity in Edinburgh has always been the boast of the right-wing, like the Save the Royal High School Campaign and the Edinburgh Amenity and Transport Association. But if you want better amenities in your ward — playgrounds, sports facilities, or maybe just a zebra crossing — or if you are fighting a council plan, mobilising can bring results. Remember, council decisions are usually rushed, often mistaken, and will crumble before determined opposition. BUT you must get in BEFORE a firm decision is officially announced. The Town Planning Department, Market Street, will give you details of all planning proposals and you must mobilise quickly. Continuous intense activity isn't necessary: the secret is timing and persistence.

Your main public weapon is organising your own demo.

For processions or marches, an organiser must give seven days

116

notice in his own hand to the Town Clerk, City Chambers, and must state the date, time, purpose and route of the march. The application is passed on to the magistrates who take advice from the Chief Constable. Strictly speaking it can be illegal for these people to meet and talk in a public place. In practice, for public meetings, contact the Chief Constable's Dept. The police can close streets to traffic, useful for protests outside US Consulate. To use public parks, apply to the Town Clerk who will contact the Civic Amenities Committee. Special permission is needed for use of loud speakers. Certain sites are set aside for public meetings in the East Meadows. Calton Hill, Inverleith Park, Saughton Park, Leith Links, Union Park, Raeburn Valley, Harrison and Cairnton Park, and best of all the Foot of the Mound.

A petition is only useful for gauging support and mobilising all people interested. First, form a compact action committee, and circulate all groups in your area for support. Ask for written statements of support from M.P.'s, Councillors and other prominent figures.

Leaflet the area, stick up posters and mount an exhibition.
Write to the newspapers, especially THE SCOTSMAN.

Try and get publicity for your problem in columns like "Action Wanted" in the EVENING NEWS, CRACKER, ROOTS; Student newspapers will be interested in your case.
weapon, so keep the media informed and time-table your action to suit their deadlines. Prepare hand-outs to feed the press with your main arguments and background material. For press contacts see 'Communications'. Well-publicised counter-information is the key to success. Research the back-ground of councillors and firms involved.

Submit a memorandum to the relevant Corporation Committee even if you don't have the support of your councillors. Contact the Town Clerk at the City Chambers (225 2424).
Send a deputation to the meeting. This is a useful focal point for protest and publicity. Demonstrations outside the City Chambers' offices of developers and business firms are the most effective setting for handing in petitions.

Direct action, like squatting, works because it attracts the press and forces the authorities to do something. But be sure of a certain amount of support before you ask people to protest in public.

## ALTERNATIVE GROUPS

Alternative political groupings fall under roughly 8 headings international, ecological, legal, personal liberation, schools, housing, Marxist and Anarchist. For details of ecological, legal, personal liberation, schools and housing, see appropriate section in this book.

The internationally-oriented groups are usually concerned with raising cash or consciousness vis-a-vis the Third World, although some, like Amnesty International have more specific objectives. The trend (at last) is away from can-rattling towards spreading understanding of how the world's economic system causes this oppression. Good material is produced, but a lot of time is spent preaching to the converted, and possibilities for action tend to be limited.

Besides world poverty, there are a number of anti-racialist groups, who have enjoyed success objectives, e.g. forcing Edinburgh University to sell its South African investments resisting the attendance of Rhodesia and South Africa to the A.C.U. Conference.

The Marxists are characterised by the belief that man's problems cannot be solved under capitalism, where economic logic of production for profit rather than needs necessitates a housing shortage, unemployment, limited education, the nuclear family, individualistic consumerism, etc. While such beliefs are also to be found within what might be termed the 'counter-culture', the Marxists differentiate themselves by the insistence that capitalism will not end by the propagation of counter-cultural ideas and projects, but by smashing the bourgeois state and creating democratic working-class control of the means of production, meaning industry, of course, but also schools, hospitals, housing estates, etc.

However, you may agree that Marx had a lot of the answers but be bewildered by the seeming plethora of groups and labels on the Marxist left. The basic division within Marxism lies between the Communists and the 'Trotskyists', — all Marxist groups will accept the designation 'Communists' or 'Marxist-Leninist': 'Stalinism' is used by Trotskyists to describe the Communist Party. This division springs from the dispute between Trotsky and Stalin after the death of Lenin in 1924. The issues which are still the important differences between C.P. and Trotskyists are: Firstly, is socialism possible within one country, or must it be international? The Communists argue (although not totally uncritically) that socialism has been built with a single state, i.e. the Soviet Union. The Trotskyists argue that if the revolution is not international, the workers' state will eventually degenerate or become state capitalist, because it will be impelled to develop bureaucratically and militaristically. Secondly, there is the question of the role of the revolutionary party in the conquest of state power. The Trotskyists hold that the fusion of party and state (single-party state) is un—Marxist, because the revolutionary aim is the 'withering—away' of the state, and there are too many great dangers involved in revolutionaries becoming bureaucrats. "Maoism" can mean one of two almost totally irreconcilable ideas—either hard-line Stalinism (e.g. Workers' Party of Scotland) or a spontaneism that even goes beyond the anarchists (e.g. Gauche Proletarianne).

Moving from right to left, we begin with the Communist Party, who are the largest group, although their members are less active than other groups. Their strategy, according to the new manifesto, lies in the election of a left-wing government which with active grass-roots working class support will socialise the means of production and dismantle the bourgeois state. Their critics on the left maintain that, in practice, Communist strategy is too much concerned with elitist politics, e.g. gaining control of Trade Union offices, at the expense of grass-roots organisations.

Other Marxist groups (Workers' Party of Scotland apart) are 'Trotskyist' (i.e. they originate in Trotsky's attack on Stalin's nationalism and his bureaucratisation of the Soviet state). Although without an Edinburgh branch, the Socialist Labour League (S.L.L.) makes itself known through Workers' Press, an almost-daily newspaper which is worth reading especially for a lot of material (Northern Ireland, police repression) which doesn't make the national press.

The International Socialists are the largest of the Trotskyist tendencies, with a branch of 70 members in Edinburgh, the majority of whom are workers. They are distinguishable from all other Marxist groups by their belief that the U.S.S.R. is a state capitalist country. At a more immediate level, they differ from S.L.L. and I.M.G. (see below) on how the revolutionary party is to be built (the S.L.L. strategy being very elitist). They produce a good weekly paper, Socialist Worker, and are invovled in work-based socialist groups, like Case Con (social workers, students) and Rank-and-File (teachers).

The International Marxist Group are a small group who

put a very strong emphasis on the intellectual aspect of being a Marxist. I.M.G. also stress the anti-imperialist revolutions, rather than the struggle in the advanced capitalist countries. They now publish 'Red Weekly', son of 'Red Mole'.

> "Scotch Liberty
> Agree
> Wi' me".

Alexander Scott

## POLITICAL PARTIES

COMMUNIST PARTY, 137 Buccleuch St., Edinburgh 8. Tel: 667-8383.

CONSERVATIVE PARTY, 11 Atholl Crescent, Edinburgh 3. Tel: 229 1342.

LABOUR PARTY, 15 Windsor Street, Edinburgh. Tel: 556 5158.

LIBERAL PARTY, 2 Atholl Place, Edinburgh, 3. Tel: 229 7484.

INTERNATIONAL SOCIALISTS: 20 Stanley Road, Edinburgh. Tel: 552 2901. Weekly paper "Socialist Worker". Edinburgh meetings advertised.

INTERNATIONAL MARXIST GROUP: British Section Fourth International. Weekly paper "Red Weekly", c/o Tim Hall, 10, Wardlow Street, Edinburgh.

SOCIALIST PARTY OF GREAT BRITAIN: c/o M. Know, 4 Sth. Elgin Street, Edinburgh. Weekly paper "Socialist Standard", meets Freegardeners Hall, Picardy Place, Mondays at 20.00

WORKERS PARTY OF SCOTLAND (Marxist—Leninist): For workers republic of Scotland. Publishes "Forth Valley Vanguard".

## ACTIVIST GROUPS

AMNESTY INTERNATIONAL: Aids victims of repression, mainly political prisoners. Waymark, 13 Comiston Road, Edin. 10.Tel : 447 5929.

ANARCHISTS: Aim to spread and apply anarchist principles. Affiliated to the Organisation of Revolutionary Anarchists. See Chris Kerr, 9 Mayfield Ter., Edin. 9. Tel: 667 2939. Weekly newspaper, "Freedom".

ANTI-APARTHEID MOVEMENT: Opposes white minority regime in Southern Africa. Sells "Anti—Apartheid News", Sec., Elizabeth Dunlop, 12 Learmonth Ter., Edinburgh 4. Tel: 332-6151.

BLACK LIBERATION FRONT: 54 Wightman Road, London, N.4. Exists to fight for black people's rights throughout the country. Monthly paper, 'Grass Roots'.

**CAS—CON:** 20 Stanley Road, Edin. Tel: 552 2901. Ask for Margaret Boushel. A socialist group for all types of social workers and social work students. Aims to develop a clearer awareness among social workers of their coercive role in our society and how they can contribute to changing it.

**FRIENDS, PEACE AND RELATIONS COMMITTEE:** Geoffrey Carnall, 145 Bruntsfield Place, Edin. EH19 4EB. Tel: 229 1124. Works to promote Quaker writings against war and racial discrimination.

**MEDICAL AID FOR VIETNAM:** Mary Cowan, Newton House, Dalkeith. Tel: 665 2817. Co-operates with the CAMPAIGN FOR PEACE VIETNAM' Organises demos, film shows, collections.

**NATIONAL CONVENTION FOR SCOTLAND:** Mary Cowan, Newton House, Dalkeith. Tel: 665 2817. Seems to co-ordinate and increase groups seeking Scottish independence. Has produced a policy document.

**OXFAM:** 80 Hanover Street, Edinburgh. Tel: 226 2856. Aims at world wide relief of starvation.

**PEOPLE:** 69 Hertford Street, Coventry, Warwickshire. Concerned with survival in all respects and improvement in the quality of life. Has no relevance to traditional 'left' or 'right' doctrines, considering all previous political movements to be the misdirected opposition.

**POVERTY ACTION GROUP:** c/o Citizens Rights Office, 11 Castle Street, Edin. Tel: 226 6349. Pressure group to highlight specific and general cases of poverty and to spread info on welfare rights.

**THIRD WORLD GROUP:** c/o International Centre, 44 Lauriston Place, Edinburgh. Organises discussions, seminars, films and talks on aspects of third world development.

**TRADES COUNCIL:** 11 Albany Street, Edin. Tel: 556 2006. Co-ordinates trade union activities. Gives details on how and which union to join.

**UNITED NATIONS ASSOCIATION:** 44 Frederick St., Edin. Promotes the public acceptance of the objectives of the UN. Organises public meetings, study groups, etc.

**UNITED NATIONS YOUTH AND STUDENT ASSOCIATION:** Youth section of UNA International Centre, 44 Lauriston Pl.

**WHITE PANTHER PARTY:** Central H.Q. (London Chapter), c/o IT. 11B Wardour Mews, London, W.1. Tel: 01-434 1372. Although an international party, accepting that national issues affect us on a day-to-day basis and have to be dealt with, a strong emphasis on 'grass roots' work.

**WORLD DEVELOPMENT MOVEMENT:** Sec., Brian Gerard, 51, Caiystane Ter., Edin. Tel: 445 2811. Aims to generate awareness of the problems of the poor countries and to press for government action.

**WOMEN'S INTERNATIONAL LEAGUE FOR PEACE AND FREE-DOM:** Dr. M.C. Marwick, 5 Northfield Cres., Edinburgh. Tel: 661-3393, Brings together women of different nationalities to study the causes of war and to work for peace and total disarmament.

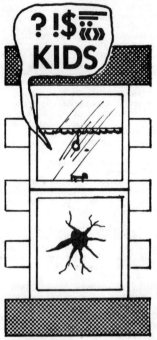

Cities are designed and built by adults for adults.

PLAY AREAS

are either too few—too far from home—or badly designed. Local authorities have a wide variety of powers to provide facilities for play but the biggest problem anyone has to face in getting things moving is APATHY, both from the corporation and from local communities. But improvements can and have been brought about in Edinburgh by such groups as Tenants Associations and Community Action Groups. (See HELP, GRASS ROOTS sections).

Here are a few ideas about what to do and how to get money.

URBAN AID PROGRAMME gives grants to socially deprived areas for the establishment of voluntary play groups, adventure playgrounds including staff, and the extention of existing play areas.

SLUM CLEARANCE SUBSIDY can provide money for temporary playgrounds in redevelopment areas.

THE NATIONAL PLAYING Fields Association 12 Manor Place 225 4307 will advise on the establishment of adventure playgrounds etc. and can offer financial assistance to approved schemes.

THE CORPORATION can provide play space after school hours and during the holidays in school playgrounds. Find out what schools in your area offer these schemes as they are often not well publicised.

In areas where there is no extra open space available, local authorities can create play streets by closing the road to vehicular traffic.

## PLAY: FREE

These areas are mostly away from home so young children unfortunately have to depend upon adults to take them. If older children are allowed to go on their own, make sure that they know the bus routes (Bus map available from Transport Headquarters, 14 Queen Street) or that they are safe on their bicycles (Contract the cycling proficiency people through your local school).

ARTHUR'S SEAT—magnificent view from the top, ducks on Duddingston Loch, sheep running free.

BLACKFORD HILL—great for sledging. Observatory open to visitors on Wednesday afternoons.

BOTANIC GARDENS, Inverleith Row—feed the squirrels, see tropical fish and flowers.

BRAID HILLS—good for kite flying and hiking.

MEADOWS—for football especially on Sunday.

MOST MUSEUMS are free. Best one for all ages is Chambers Street.

FIRE ENGINE MUSEUM, McDonald Road, where children are allowed to climb on the engines.

PRINCES STREET GARDENS have free variety shows (punch and Judy) during the summer.

There are 3 adventure playgrounds in Edinburgh that provide a wide range of indoor and outdoor activities—well worth a visit.

NIDDRIE ADVENTURE PLAYGROUND Niddrie Mains Terr. 661 4304.

LEITH, Linksview area.

SCOTLAND YARD set up in old Railway Station.

## CLUBS, WORKSHOP, LIBRARY

THEATRE WORKSHOP, Hanover Street (at the moment of writing they were looking for new premises) Ph. 226 6808. Fantastic place where kids over 5 can try sculpting, painting, acting, acrobatics, photography etc. Costs £2 for a 10 week term.

CENTRAL CHILDRENS LIBRARY, George IV Bridge. Free. Picture stories for the under fives. Library club which operates on certain evenings after school hours does all sorts of exciting things like mask competitions.

YOUTH CLUBS. Lists available from Edinburgh Youth Handbook published free by Edinburgh Corporation Education Dept. St. Giles Street.

## SPORTS & EQUIPMENT

SWIMMING. If you want to swim in the sea its best to go out of Edinburgh. There are some nice beaches down the east coast.

ROYAL COMMONWEALTH POOL is the best pool. Costumes can be hired and the water is warm, also provides playpens for nuisance younger brothers.

Try PORTOBELLO open air pool on warm days.

MURRAYFIELD ICE RINK, & HAYMARKET costs 9p plus the skates. See local paper for times.

JUDO Club at Hillside Crescent. Costs about £3 a term.

TENNIS COURTS. Corporation ones—20p for 40 minutes. Rackets and balls can be hired. Woman in the Meadows are super.

TRAMPOLINE CENTRE. Phone 669 1075 for details.

FOOTBALL fans can get shown round the football grounds in Edinburgh and can watch the training sessions. HIBS Phone 661 2159, for HEARTS Phone 337 6132. For your own football gear Ronnie, Simpson, Rose Street.

MEADOWBANK SPORTS CENTRE, 139 London Road run a lot of schemes that are well worth finding out about.

CYCLING at Meadowbank on Sundays for over 10.

For cycling equipment try

HYDES, St. Leonards, old fashioned bike shop.

BIKE SHOP, Preston Street often has some good bargains in second hand bikes.

HALFORDS for toddler trikes and bike accessories.

For second hand equipment try Jumble Sales and the junk shop in Lothian Street.

McKENZIES, S.Bridge have the best range of all types of sports stuff.

### See PEOPLE AT WORK

If you can get a few friends together then with an adult, you can be shown round all sorts of places

SCOTSMAN Offices, North Bridge see around the big presses that turn out the newspapers.

STV Studios, Gateway, Leith Walk. Those over 12 can sit in on a show and see around afterwards, those under 12 just see the studios. Write to the Controller Mr. McPherson first to arrange a time. ETC.

The ZOO is out at Corstorphine and costs 15p for children (adults 35p), but you can make a whole day of it. Feeding times from 2 pm—don't miss the chimps tea party. Pony rides at the Childrens' Farm.

MUSEUM OF CHILDHOOD, High Street, costs 5p see toys throughout the ages.

ODEON CINEMA, Nicholson Street shows childrens matinees throughout the school holidays. Nice on a rainy afternoon.

For more ideas see Edinburgh For Children issued by the Morningside Parent Teachers Association 2nd Edition re-issue late autumn or contact Mrs. Kilbrey, 15 Cluny Avenue, Edinburgh 10.

# KIDS KONSUMER

## Clothes

MOTHERCARE, Princes Street is the best place for baby's clothes.

CHARITY SHOPS (see Things) especially BRUNTSFIELD BABY SHOP, 22 Bruntsfield Place for 2nd hand clothes.

For free baby gear like prams etc. get in contact with the social worker in the maternity hospital when you book in. They can often (not always) get prams and cots from Barnardoes provided they are returned, and money for nappies from special funds that they know about.

SQUARE DEAL PRAM CO. Bread Street. Hire and repair of baby equipment.

Children's clothes
Most head shops sell kids stuff—see Things
Also—

C & A, cheap, lots of tricel rubbish but some wearable items. Advantage of lots of running and trying on space for toddlers.

MARKS & SPENCERS, very crowded, avoid Saturdays when shopping with the children. Easy to change articles that don't fit.

ARMY & NAVY Stores throughout the city best buys for heavy duty stuff.

BURROWS and PARKERS for very cheap things.

SCHOOL EXCHANGE, 42 George Street, for school clothes

## TOYS & MODELS

PLEGA, High Street, wealth of ideas but expensive.

GALT Toy Shop, Scotch House, Princes Street, same type of stuff plus lots of outdoor toys like swings, slides, climbing frames.

WONDERLAND Toy Centre, Rose Street, Models and Toys.

HARBURN HOBBIES, 124 Leith Walk and CAPITAL MODELS, Canongate, for models.

TOYCRAFT, top of Leith Walk for cheap stuff. Good for mechanical toys.

DOLLS BOUTIQUE, Leith Walk, everything for the trendy doll.

STRACHAN'S DOLLS HOSPITAL, 23 Dalry Road. Also great for jokes and tricks.

Second hand toys can be picked up cheap at Jumble Sales—see local newspapers.

## BOOKS

Can be borrowed at the Children's Library.

Exchanged at D.L's book exchange which also deal with old comic books.

THINS of the Bridges have the best range of childrens books. Ask for the legendary Mrs. Granger.

BETTER BOOKS, Forrest Road. Nice kids books and French books.

## ARTS & CRAFTS

best go to real art shops.

GREYFRIARS Art Shop, 1 Greyfriars Place for art material.

AITKEN DOTT, Castle Street, art materials

ALEXANDERS, Newington Road for all sorts of craft stuff—tissue papers, moulds, leatherwork.

SMITHS, Frederick Street for needlework, embroidery and felt.

## PETS

There are a great deal of problems involved in keeping pets in the city. First of all find out if you are allowed to keep a pet in your house, some landladies and sometimes the Corporation won't allow them.

The SSPCA, 19 Melville Street Phone 225 6418 provide a 24 hour emergency service seven days a week for any problems that crop up. This group also provides free literature for children that deals with the care of all types of pets.

TO BUY

AQUARAMA, Leith Walk has an amazing tank of fish. Ask the man about them and he'll talk for hours.

PET SHOP, Fleshmarket Close have all types of pets.

PET SHOP, Salisbury Place, for hamsters and mice.

GIBSONS of Clerk Street for pet food.

We're made to believe that kids are "deprived" and have a bad start in life unless they start their educational career at the age of 3. A lot of public money is spent on nursery classes providing "part-time places", and playgroups, although it is obvious that the provision for the needy is totally inadequate. There is a "priority" waiting list of 500 to get day nursery places and it's difficult to get a full-time nursery-school place.

Modern city life is hardly ideal for young kids, but there are lots of things kids can do at home and round about town (see KIDS section). Generally children are no better off going to nurseries or playgroups, unless it's necessary.

If you do need or want to send your kid, make sure you like the place and get on well with the people who run it, otherwise your kid is unlikely to benefit.

## EDUCATION AND CARE FOR THE UNDER-FIVES

Preschool education is "in", but confusing because of the different kinds of places, run either by the Corporation or privately, that provide it. If you want to send your kids, these are the places you can choose from:

# DAY NURSERIES

CORPORATION (Social Work Department): 14 nurseries: 800 places; hours: 8 am—6 pm; cost: 7p—£1.25/day according to income; age: 0—5 years. Information from Social Work Department, 14 Castle Terr., tel: 229 7541 (Miss Brown).

Day nurseries are for people who cannot possibly look after their kids themselves. It is virtually impossible to get a place unless you're single or in real trouble and even then it may be hard. Your kids will be cared for well physically, but that's all they can afford to offer. If possible, put your kid into a NURSERY SCHOOL when he/she is 3.

PRIVATE: 61 childminders are registered with the Social Work Department. They look after 2 or 3 kids at the time for about £1 a day. The Social Work Department publishes a list.

The University runs the day nurseries for kids of students and staff. They're more expensive than the Corporation ones, but you'll have a better chance of getting a place.

# NURSERY SCHOOLS AND CLASSES

CORPORATION (Education Department): 16 schools + 44 classes attached to primary schools (3000 places): hours: full time 9 am—3.(30) pm; part time: 9—12 am; 1—3.30 pm; cost: 60p a week for school dinners (if you can afford them) and voluntary contributions; age: 3—5 years old. Information from: Education Department, St. Giles St., Edinburgh 1. Tel: 225 2424.

A lot of new nursery classes have been opened during the last few years, which means you should have little trouble in getting a part-time place. Full time places are pretty hard to get and you'd be wise to get on to a waiting list at least a year in advance.

Nursery education is very undefined with the result that some schools and classes are really good, others really bad.

PRIVATE Nurseries and Playgroups registered with Social Work Department: 160 nurseries and playgroups: hours: appx. 9:30—12, some also 1:30—3:30; cost: around 5p/day; age: 2—5 years. Information from Social Work Department, 14 Castle Terr. (Mrs. Macaulay) and PreSchool Playgroups Association, 304 Maryhill Road, Glasgow N.W.

Playgroups are increasing in number and popularity, though their value is questionable., if you want more than just a short break from your kid every day. Alternatively you may want to get involved in running it, which may be useful if you feel cut off or lonely.

You can set up your own playgroup in a public building or in your own house, but it is a complicated business. Playgroups have to be registered with the Social Work Department and need to satisfy rules and regulations about facilities and staffing. The Corporation does however provide some money to get you started.

# Schools

Labour-controlled Edinburgh is going comprehensive, but that's unlikely to make much difference to the city's class ridden educational system. Selective Royal High was the first school to restake its place in a solidly middle-class area, Barnton, and a recently opened comprehensive at Redford had only a handful of middle-class kids. Bussing may be a future problem but generally the city's sharply differentiated social structure defines the class basis of its educational intake.

Every available type of school is here—independent, grant-aided, corporation, selective, comprehensive, Catholic—even a Catholic comprehensive girls' school—yet Edinburgh spends less on education per person than any other area bar the Scilly Isles. The fee-paying schools, protected by aggressive parents' committees, are bad: there are more pupils per teacher there than in corporation schools.

Taking secondary schools of all kinds—local authority, local authority fee-paying, grant aided, independent—about 23% of all their first year intake is in fee-paying schools. In their fourth year ('O' grade year) this rises to 40%; in the fifth year ('H' grade year) 60%; in their sixth year, 75% of all sixth year children are in fee-paying schools, The conclusions hardly require spelling out; the class picture that emerges, the educational affront and direct deprivation to those 25% non-fee paying pupils who stay on to that stage.

As for changes within schools, not much hope here either. 'Streaming' or the system of stunting the child with official expectations is the norm even in Edinburgh's state schools.


### Alternative Education

Alternative education involves a radical break with traditional schooling, which the comprehensive idea is not. Good education means encouraging the individual child to develop in his given tastes and interests, and this requires a much better teacher/child ratio. It should also be rooted in the cultural environment of the child, making sense of the life his community leads,—not an academic leap into an alien knowledge. But the establishment that controls educational policy isn't widely keen on real history or real politics, or even real science, except in a narrow technocratic a political sense. For real alternative education (apart from the free learning every child imbibes **outside** school hours) we must look to free,schools.

## Free Schools

There are no Free School in Edinburgh yet, though legally there is little to hinder them. An independent school is defined as one not under the management of an education authority, receiving no direct grant from SED and having at least five pupils of compulsory school age. Almost any person may act as 'proprietor' in the independent school category.

For full legal information on setting up your own school, contact Alison Truefitt, 73 Highbury New Park, London N5, or the NCCL, 152 Camden High Street, London NW1.

There exist two main examples for anyone who's thinking of starting a free school. Firstly there's those like the Kirkdale school at Sydenham (778 0149) which charges fees (kept as low as possible and adjusted to parents' means) and pays its teachers. Then there's the Scotland Rd. School in Liverpool, based in a working-class area where there are no fees, and teachers live off Social Security. Here they involve the local unemployed and run jumble sales, raffles etc. to raise funds.

In Glasgow Barrowfield Community School opened at the beginning of June 1973 with one teacher and seven pupils. Other teachers are prepared to join as the number of pupils increases.

Free schools are really worth supporting either by sending your kids to one or starting one yourself. Even if they don't directly cause the straight system to wither away, they do show what can be done, if we get education out of bureaucratic hands. This in itself can stimulate the demand for community control of education.

## Open University

The only alternative in the higher education sector at the

moment—and disappointing to many expectations. Theoretically, it's open to everyone on a first come, first served basis but it's unfortunate that most of those taking up its opportunities tend to have educational qualifications already (teachers, civil servants etc.). Judgment of your ability is based upon a mixture of straight exams and continuous assessment. Local authority grants are available for summer school fees and travelling expenses—apply to the Education Dept. in St. Giles St. For local Open University enquiries, phone 226 3851.

**Scotch Education**

'I tellt ye
I tellt ye'.

Alexander Scott

## University and Edinburgh

Ten years ago the then Principal of Edinburgh University announced a new relationship between the University and the city of Edinburgh. We were to have "the university in the city and the city in the university". With ten thousand students and half that number of academic and non-academic employees, the University is the second largest property developer and one of the largest landowners and employers in the city. The University gets a lot out of Edinburgh — but it often appears that the city gets little from the university. Under present expansion plans, which include the redevelopment of the Nicholson Street area four thousand residents — half the population of the University area — will have been removed by 1981 and the University already proposes to expand along Lauriston Place with a new Dental School. One of the results is that various groups are now pressing to expand out of the centre and in less densely populated areas.

The University does permit a number of mature students over twenty-five to study at the university — there are perhaps five hundred at the most — but they usually require at least three good Higher grade passes. In association with other adult education agencies, the University also runs evening classes, but these have been criticised as a "middle class alternative to bingo". Fees one term £1.10, 2 terms £1.90, 3 terms £2.60. Full information and booklet from the Department of Educational Studies, 11 Buccleuch Pl., or the City Education Department, 12 St. Giles St.

Radicals within the University have been pressing for more imaginative links between the university and the community. They want the University to run a Community Service Unit whereby the architectural, sociological, planning and medical expertise of the university is put free at the service of local community groups and they want the adult education services to be revamped on a community basis to run courses held in pubs and so on in all city districts and grounded in the problems of city life. Other plans have been for the University to provide resources for at least one thousand adult local residents to enrol in full time courses at the University without the necessary qualifications and for the buildings, equipment and the resources of the University to be offered at night, at weekends and out of term time to local societies, groups and individuals to use as they wish.

### Further Education

Classes at the four further education colleges in Edinburgh are open to everyone. If your employer is sending you on a course he is generally responsible for your fees for enrolment, exams and membership of the student association. Get every penny you're entitled to: the boss isn't sending you there for your own good as much as his own. The colleges are all new, well equipped and generally staffed by good teachers:

Napier College, Colinton Rd. (447 1011). Mostly higher degree and diploma work (CNAA, HND) with 165 courses available both day and evening. There is an interesting education technology side and a Learning By Appointment Centre (phone and ask for extension 21 for further information).

Stevenson College, Bankhead Ave., Sighthill (433 7111). Offers a wide number of classes, particularly on the secretarial side, and does 'O', 'H' and 'A' Levels in many general subjects including sciences; also offers ONCs in Chemistry and Physics on an evening basis. Fairly extensive language facilities.

Edinburgh College of Commerce, Sighthill Court (433 6061). Offers a BSc in economics, making it the only place outside the universities to get a degree other than science. Other than that it's very much a commercial college with evening courses available in business studies and wide secretarial courses.

Telford College, Crewe Toll (332 7631). There's no indication what the raising of the school leaving age will do to Telford's one year school leaver's course, but it's worth enquiring if you're interested—apparently it's possible to get bursaries for these. Also evening courses in Highers and 'O' levels, commercial subjects and engineering. Extensive Dept. of Hairdressing.

## Other Courses

The Corporation publishes a booklet, **Guide to Recreation and Leisure Time Activities,** the only comprehensive guide to the incredible number of courses offered by organisations in the city (it's a shame that every ratepayer isn't sent a copy each year). The city is divided into 5 regions, each with its own tutors and centres:

East: Portobello Adult Education Centre, Duddingston Rd. (669 6304).

North-East: Leith Adult Centre, Duncan Pl. (554 1059).

North-West: Craigmount Adult Education Centre, Craigs Rd. (334 8278).

South-East: Gracemount Adult Education Centre, Lasswade Rd. (664 4818).

South-West: Firrhill Adult Education Centre, Firrhill (441 1031)

**Other than the Corporation you can try:**

The Workers' Educational Association (WEA), 13 Abercromby Pl. (556 6913). Isn't as working-class as it sounds (quite a few tories among its lecturers). Their list is wide and the series last for 16 lectures at a cost of £1.90.

Basil Paterson, 22 Abercromby Pl. (556 7695). The last of the old 'crammers'—does everything from common entrance to 1st year degree cramming (also runs a summer course in English for foreign students). Private tuition is expensive ('O' level and Higher, £1.80 an hour; 1st year degree £2.20). Small classes also.

**Useful Addresses:**

EDINBURGH AND MID LOTHIAN ASSOCIATION FOR THE ADVANCEMENT OF STATE EDUCATION, c/o Brian Elliot, 32 Argyle Cres., Edin. (669 5811).

LIBERTARIAN TEACHERS ASSOCIATION, c/o Peter Ford, 22 Royal Road, Ramsgate, Kent.

PRE-SCHOOL PLAYGROUPS ASSOCIATION, Mrs. J. Gibb, 15 South Gillsland Rd. (447 3105).

RANK AND FILE, c/o Sheila Gilmore, 17 Hillside St.   Left wing members of N.U. Teachers.

NATIONAL UNION OF SCHOOL STUDENTS, c/o Ian Mackay, 1 Northfield Cres., Longridge, West Lothian.   Schools' branch of N.U. Students.

SCHOOLS ACTION UNION, Box 19, Roots, 6 Lonsdale Terr. Fighting for democratic control of schools.

A relatively high unemployment rate is a fact of life in Edinburgh. This is exacerbated by the nature of the capital itself, with its low industrialisation, its emphasis on tourism, its resident disproportionate quota of professional and retired persons, and a predominant philosophy of political consensus. The effect is one of tangible socio-economic discrimination: Edinburgh's population declines

134

at a rate of around 2,000 per annum, and by far the largest percentage who are leaving are the young and the working classes who cannot find jobs and who, even if they are employed, can't get suitable accommodation. This contrasts sharply with the increasing inflow of tourists each year. Edinburgh literally exports its problems and imports its wealth.

Current trends, and your chances of finding a job here are best summarised by the following table of unemployment figures for Edinburgh, Leith and Portobello.

|  | Male | Female | Total |
|---|---|---|---|
| June 1968 | 3739 | 560 | 4299 |
| June 1969 | 4308 | 532 | 4840 |
| June 1970 | 5798 | 702 | 6500 |
| June 1971 | 7453 | 856 | 8309 |
| June 1972 | 7414 | 1093 | 8507 |
| June 1973 | 7657 | 1110 | 8767 |

Even the breakdown of employment figures for Edinburgh betrays the nature of the city itself—six of the top ten employers in terms of numbers are occupations which are either wholly or largely of a middle-class nature. The educations services come out top with 18,464 employees (June 1970), while 'industries' like medical and dental services, insurance and banking and bill discounting also rank highly.

## WHERE TO LOOK FOR HELP

Edinburgh has two alternative work agencies. HELP info service (tel: 554 6908) has set up an alternative work agency, Gentle Ghost style, for those who can't or won't fit into the 9—5 routine.

CITIZENS' RIGHTS Office at 11 Castle Street is also gathering and systematising info on jobs mainly with the aim of helping middle-aged unemployed and disabled as much as the young.

If they can't help the 'Evening News' has a good Jobs Vacant and Jobs Wanted section each day and the 'Scotsman' is worth a look for 'professional appointments'. Students should try the SRC Vac Emp Centre in Chambers

St. and notice-boards in Students' Unions and Shops.

If all these fail, you could always try DEP Labour Exchange—you never know.

Whatever happens, realise if you resort to a commercial work agency you are being exploited. Their standard method is to act as middleman, paying you so much themselves and charging your employer so much more for your services. Fairly typical is that the agency's 'cut' of the fee paid for your services is about one-third. One resultant disadvantage is that the agency-employee finds him or herself earning considerably less than other company employees doing the same job.

## WHERE TO FIND A JOB

These are mostly suggestions for temporary work, but if you make out well in a job there's a fair chance you can stay on longer. The national economic situation is important when applying for work in the big organised industries—if times are tough the unions are likely to oppose temporary workers.

THE CORPORATION: A refuse-collector gets a basic wage of around £21 and occasional overtime. Women are often used for waste-paper collection—wage £19. There are few perks—tips are rare and crews usually share proceeds of any scrap metal or valuables found. Street orderly is a lighter job, but for men only— expect around £19 and watch out for plain-clothes corporation spies. For these apply to the Corporation Cleansing Dept., Kings Stables Rd. (225 2424). Good places to try for open-air jobs, in parks, swimming pools and beaches in the summer are the Parks & Recreation Dept. in York Place (225 2424) and the Baths & Laundries Dept., Dalkeith Rd. Pool attendants and beach patrollers receive a basic wage of £19, plus lots of overtime and a free swim any time, while work in parks brings in around £18. A more morbid occupation, but not seasonal, is grave-digging—wage £18. Finally, school janitor is a nice job if you can get it, especially in the summer when school's out—£23 a week—apply to the Education Dept., Edinburgh Corporation.

CARS: If you have your own car or van there's lots of money to be made. With your own van you can advertise yourself locally as a removal service—charging around £1 an hour. If you know the city and surroundings well you can set yourself up for guided tours or become sub-contracted to a tourist agency—make £5 a day clear profit plus good tips on this. Minibus hire is another profitable idea, but don't expect your phone to be ringing constantly. For drivers with a clean licence, ice-cream vans are not the only hope, but good jobs are hard to come by. Delivering new cars to purchasers—try the big car salerooms. Life on the buses is a good line for increasing nervous tension (shift and overtime work but pays £18.50 basic, though they won't take on temporary staff) and the GPO looks for extra drivers at Christmas (£23+ and plenty of overtime). If you are mechanically minded advertise yourself for car repairs, and for the completely uninitiated there's always the lonely, lowly-paid vigil at the all-night or late-night petrol pump. Finally, the big 'con': order the latest model of a rare but much sought car, reserving the right to cancel. If delivery is slow and a waiting list grows, you can 'earn' anything from £10-£100 by advertising the car in a reputable paper when it's ready for delivery: many people are willing to pay for the advantage of not waiting. The snag is you either have to look or sound respectable and wealthy before the firm accepts your order.

SECURITY:  If you don't mind para-military organisations or guarding the bastions of capitalism, you earn good money working very long hours for firms like Securicor, Security Express, Group 4 Factory Guards and Sentry Securities. They are looking for people they can trust—expect to be vetted. Type of work ranges from static guards on sites to crew men on cash vehicles. Lots of part-time work. Average basic wage for a 50+ hour week is around £28. A possible way of earning a lot quickly in the summer when big events are coming off.

MODELLING:  Joan Donald in Murrayfield Rd. (337 4565) is probably the best place to try for commercial modelling. They're looking for all types of looks and figures. Snags are that you have to take a course which you pay for, they will take a commission on earnings, and you get paid months behind. If you do make it, though, you can earn a lot of casual irregular work. Other than that, apply to the Art College, Lauriston Pl. (229 4472). There's usually a waiting list there, but they use around 10 to 15 models per week at 50p an hour.

SPECIAL EVENTS:  Big events like fetes, gala days and open-air shows are always lucrative. The Edinburgh Festival (late Aug.—early Sept.) is a bonanza for good temporary jobs, apart from increased possibilities in busking, catering services, hotel work and ticket touting, there are enjoyable jobs in stagework and scenery shifting—get a copy of the Frings brochure in advance and contact the groups and theatres concerned offering your services. Money depends on the size and/or success of the group and is often fairly low, but perks are association with 'stardom', some free food and accommodation and plenty of parties. 'Official' Festival theatres are probably the best places for jobs like programme-selling, ticket collection or seat-ushering. There are also many publications around to sell to pubs and theatre crowds—Infringe, Alternative Edinburgh, New Edinburgh Review, the Pub Guide (for all these apply to 1 Buccleuch Pl. (667 5718), Cracker, Roots and Scottish International.  For the literary-minded there is a chance of making unofficial 'royalties' by

137

reading or selling your poetry to Festival crowds—the Traverse and the Pool among others hold regular meetings. Or simply rent out your flat during the Festival—apply to the Fringe Club.

Keep your eye open also for events such as the Royal Highland Show (mid-June), the Scottish Horse Show (August), the Edinburgh Highland Games (mid-August) and the various exhibitions and sporting events in Edinburgh throughout the year. There is always work there as gateman, programme-seller, general labourer etc., though many of the bigger jobs are sub-contracted out by the organisers. For big events locally the Milk Marketing Board usually have stalls with 'dolly girls'—apply to the Sales Dept., Underwood Rd., Paisley (041 887 1234). Catering firms might be interested also—Harwell's of Colinton employ lots of temporary labour for dishwashing, serving food etc. and pay by the hour, around 30p. Tent and marquee hire services like Purvis Equipment, 9 Portland Pl. sometimes hire temps—expect little more than 35p an hour, but plenty of overtime (anything up to a 100 hour week). Finally, National Car Parks Ltd., c/o Turnhouse Airport take summer staff to deal with big events.

BREWERIES: Usually conveyor belt work—boring but not heavy. Skilled and semi-skilled do the actual beermaking. Women used for bottling. Men can expect to load and unload lorries, clean kegs etc. Shift work, but perks are nice smells and free beer. Average wage is around £28-£29. Women Less.

FACTORIES: Not recommended. Early starts and monotonous work, for anything from £13 a week. Ask around the Sighthill Industrial Estate—Burton's Gold Medal Biscuits, for instance, are often looking for people.

BUILDING SITES: Not much chance here because of a high unemployment rate in building. The best way is to ask around the foremen on the sites rather than the offices. Get in at the beginning of a contract if you can.

CONSUMER: Firms like Kleen-E-ze are always looking for door-to-door salesmen, and there's a furniture shop in Infirmary St. that employs sandwich-board advertisers. Best bets for general shopwork are tourist shops (e.g. Tartan Gift Shops) during the summer, while the big stores like C & A and Marks and Spencers are often looking for temporary and Saturday staff. There are plenty of smaller shops, cafes and restaurants with a big turnover of staff—try Sher's Little Superstore in Fowler Terr. and restaurants like the Eurasian and the Woodville.

IN THE COUNTRY: Sunshine (sometimes) and health while you work. Jobs in agriculture are getting scarcer every year, with the introduction of new seeds and the Common Market not helping much. Potato inspecting (July and August) is the best deal. bringing in up to £50 per week with wages and fiddles. Apply to the Department of Agriculture & Fisheries. The snag is that you have to take an unpaid training course for a few weeks in June, and there's a high failure rate. For potato-rogueing—again you need qualifications—it's best to set up your own cooperative or firm, but for this you need farm contacts and a lot of experience. It's not easy to get work with a rogueing firm, but try Edinburgh & District Rogueing Services, 29 Roseneath Terr. Expect £20-25 a week from a firm. Potato picking (starting off in Ayrshire in early summer and moving to East Lothians later) brings in less—around 30-35p an hour. Look for ads in the Evening News or ask round the bigger potato merchants, like Easton's, Fulton's and J & E England, and individual farmers.

Berry-picking at Blairgowrie is fun, but you'll be paid according to the weight picked—apply to Smedley's Factory.

If you're around on the 'Glorious Twelfth' (August) till late September and you're not a nature lover, try grouse-beating for the gentlemen of Argyll and Perthshire. Here you can expect free youth-hostel type of accommodation, but you supply your own weatherproof clothing and wages are subject to weather (expect around £2-3 a day).

Finally, there's general farm labour on surrounding farms. Free accommodation, rree food and lousy money. Work always required during the trade holidays and harvest-time (Sept.—Oct.)

> Know thy enemy.
>   He does not care what colour you are
>     provided you work for him;
>       he does not care how much you earn
>         provided you earn more for him;
>           he does not care who lives in the room at the top
>             provided he owns the buiding;
>               he will let you say whatever you like against him
>             provided you do not act against him;
>           he sings the praises of humanity
>         but knows machines cost more than men;
>       bargain with him he laughs and beats you at it;
>     challenge him
>   and he kills;
> sooner than lose the things he owns
>     he will destroy the world.
>
>                                     'RED MOLE'

## OFF-BEAT WORK

HELP: Alternative work agency. Phone them at 554 6908 and offer your talents.

GUINEA-PIGS FOR RESEARCH: Try the Citizens' Rights Office, university depts. (especially Science and Social Science) and university notice-boards. The Dept. of Psychiatry, Royal Edinburgh Hospital, is well-renowned for this type of work. Fairly good pay for no effort.

WRITING LETTERS: Newspapers and magazines. Judge the readership you're writing for (e.g. the Sunday Post goes in for exploding haggis and old-time reminiscences). Popular dailies and Sundays pay from 50p upwards for published correspondence. The big pay-out comes from the Reader's Digest.

**FILM & TV EXTRAS:** **Definitely not a glamorous life.** The big snag is that to get work you must join EQUITY, the actors' union (65 Bath St., Glasgow—041 332 1669), but to join you first need a contract of employment. The solution is to get a job first and say your union card is on the way. Drama students get automatic membership, irregular work, but fun if you don't take it seriously. For both BBC and ITV apply to the Glasgow studios.

**TIPPING OFF NEWSPAPERS:** Most papers pay for a tip-off on a good story. If it's a fire or an accident, phone in quickly before someone else does. If it's a scandal do the research yourself as quickly as you can, then 'sell' it.

**STREET ART:** There's a temporary art 'Gallery' on the Scotsman steps, off the Bridges, during the Festival. You can count on a fairly undiscriminating and generous viewer at that time. Otherwise forget it—you'll have to apply for a licence for display on public property, and that won't be granted in Edinburgh.

**STREET THEATRE:** This won't be allowed in the city which is so proud of its Festival drama: you'll either be moved on or charged with obstruction. Apply to the Parks Dept. as a parks entertainment—they're less stringent.

**GO-GO GIRLS:** Try the discotheques. In pubs they'll ogle at first but pretty soon get engrossed in their pints. If you just want to dance, best stick to the pubs in the city centre.

**SELLING PROGRAMMES:** At football matches and rugby internationals. A few hours work gets you free entrance to the game and enough left for a pie and a few pints.

**CINEMAS:** Always looking for usherettes and ice-cream girls. A world of darkness, but you get a free torch to light your way and free movies—again and again.

**RAGS:** Friends and babies always have old clothes. It might be worth more than a balloon to you. See to any of the shops in the Cowgate.

**COOKING:** Advertise yourself locally. Offer to do shopping, cooking and washing up and you can charge 50p-£1 a head.

**CRAFTS:** Sell your own work to friends and shops, or hire a stall in one of the markets—Cockburn St. or Greyfriars.

**TUTORING** schoolkids for Highers and 'O' levels brings in good money (£1-£1.50 an hour). Advertise or ask at your university or college SRC.

**ADVERTISING:** Offer your services in getting ads for any of the smaller local papers. You'll get good commission but it can mean a lot of wasted energy.

**SELL** this book—guarantees interesting conversations.

Finally, if you don't get a job, make sure you do get the social benefits due to you.

## TRADE UNIONS

If you do get a job it might be well worthwhile to join the union.

The transport and engineering unions, the T&GWU and the AUEW, have good reputations for pushing the claims of their memberships. By contrast the other major general union, the NUGMW (municipal workers) is not noted for its efforts in this respect. The T&GWU have recently taken an interest in recruiting hotel and bar staffs, who suffer more than most from low rates and long hours.

In the State sector the public employees union, NUPE, has a good record locally, while the building trades union, UCAAT, and the T&GWU have recently been active for better pay and conditions for general labourers.

Some useful addresses are:
EDINBURGH TRADES COUNCIL, 11 Albany St. (556 3006)
T&GWU, 18 Claremont Cres. (556 9676)
UCAAT, 1 Hillside Cres. (556 1482)
AUEW, 1 Hillside Cres. (556 4326)
NUPE, 18 Albany St. (556 7927)

## TRAINING & RETRAINING FOR WORK

Redundencies and changes in technology are increasingly demanding that workers be retrained during their working lives; to meet this the government have set up Government Training Centres throughout the country (two in the Edinburgh area)—this applies whether you are employed at present or not. Grants are given—the lowest being £11 per week for a single man with no dependents, but rates rise according to family size and are often earnings-related for those who are getting time off work for the course. If interested apply to the Training Officer of your local Employment Exchange. A word of warning—there's a waiting list for entry (if you say you're willing to accept a 48 hour allocation you get in earlier).

## AID

Social and medical benefits are your right, not charity hand-outs, so never be reticent about claiming for them. Every human being deserves an adequate standard of living and whatever the reason the so-called Welfare State was brought into being, it should be used to its fullest extent as part of any attempt to make authority realise that it is dealing with people not dehumanised machines. What follows is an outline of your most basic rights, social and medical.

# SUPPLEMENTARY BENEFITS

Anyone without a job can claim supplementary benefit as it is non-contributory and you don't need any National Insurance stamps to be eligible. However, the **Department of Health and Social Security** usually require you to sign on once a week as available for work at the **Department of Employment**. You are officially allowed 2 weeks holiday per year (on full supplementary benefit pay, no less). Those normally excused from signing are unsupported mothers and those in receipt of disability pensions. Remember that supplementary benefits are mans-tested and payments are calculated according to your resources rather than your needs. The basic grants are intended to raise your weekly income to a fixed minimum, "the Supplementary Benefits level" which is the absolute minimum amount you can bring in each week and survive.

## HOW TO CLAIM

It is necessary after registering for work to obtain a B.1. claim form from the **Department of Employment**. Ask for this and get them to fill it in for you as they usually 'forget' to tell you about it. Ask which Social Security Office serves your area and take the B.1. there, which will be one of the following:

ARGYLE HOUSE, CASTLE TERRACE;
MARITIME HOUSE, 66 SHORE, LEITH;
HAYMARKET, CLIFTON TERRACE;
PORTOBELLO, 21 WINDSOR PLACE.

If you are in urgent need of money insist on an interview. Its your legal right to be interviewed in the office, so don't be brushed off by the reception clerk who will normally try to get rid of about one third of his clients by simply advising you that 'you must have a home visit before benefit'. This is a lie: under Section 13 of the 1916 Social Security Act they are empowered to make emergency payments over the counter or more often through the post but it is not normal practice. Let them know you are aware of this.

All the Social Security offices now have appointments

143

systems — the main difference being that whereas before you had to wait up to 2 hours for an interview you now have to wait for up to 2 hours for an appointment for an interview usually within the next couple of days. Try to be punctual as you'll just have to go through the whole discouraging process again (punctual to them means at least 5 minutes early). The best times of the day to visit are 9.30 in the morning, (you'll have to wait ½ hour) or 3.25 pm as they close the doors at 3.30 pm and have to deal with everybody in the room before they can go home.

When in the interview booth its advisable and quite legal to take a witness as there are cases where claimants have been misled about their rights. If this happens a complaint to the Regional Controller, Argyle House, Lady Lawson Street, usually brings prompt action. You have a right to demand a written assessment form. A124A, detailing the exact allocation of your supplementary allowance so that you can see at a glance if you're underpaid. Don't leave the cubicle until you're satisfied as they cannot physically remove you, but on the other hand don't let them provoke you into any action which may be construed by them and the police as a breach of the peace — you have a perfect legal right to be

## RATES

Any single person directly responsible to a landlord for rent should receive £6.55 plus rent allowances (usually less than £4). A married or cohabiting couple should receive £10.65 plus rent allowance. Someone living in another person's household (e.g. with parents) and not directly responsible for rent, will receive £5.20 plus a minimum of 70p rent.

|  | Age | Rate |
|---|---|---|
|  | 18 or over | £5.20 |
|  | 16—17 | £4.05 |
| Children | 13—15 | £3.40 (parent must claim) |
|  | 11—12 | £2.75 |
|  | 5—10 | £2.25 |
|  | under 5 | £1.90 |

If you want to know what you're entitled to, demand an S.1, obtainable from 'occasional' post offices.

A person directly responsible to a landlord is understood to be a person who holds a rent book and if you are one of a group of say, 4 people, living in a flat, paying equal rent and only receiving a non-householder's scale rate of £5.20 you should appeal.

## APPEALS

If you're dissatisfied with your allowance obtain an appeal form (Form A21). Word the appeal carefully as the S.S. "prosecutor" has to read your version out in full to the appeal tribunal. Before the hearing (at **Meldrum House, Drumsheugh Gardens**), they will send you a copy of your appeal form plus their own "defence", stating the grounds they have for refusing you. From this you can work out what to say at the tribunal. Most appeals when carefully worded beforehand succeed. If you are unsure of exactly what to say, contact the **Citizens Rights Office, 11 Castle Street (226 6347)**, open Mon., Wed. and Fri. 5—8 pm, and Tues. and Thurs. 2—5 pm.

## STRIKERS AND THE S.S.

Under Section 10 of the Social Security Act, a striker is not allowed to claim for himself, but only for his dependants. If you're single and attempt to claim while on strike, you will normally be informed that you are disqualified under Section 10. However, Section 13 — the urgent needs section — empowers them to make payments if you prove that you are in urgent need (food, rent, mortgage interest payments, etc.). For married strikers the rates are £5.20 for your wife plus dependents allowances, rent and rates in full, less family allowance and any strike pay over £1. It might be worthwhile persuading your union to curtail your strike pay to £1 as you will receive the same amount in any case and this will help to reinforce your strike). Organise a Strike Claimants Union to press for your rights, especially those of single strikers.

## CO—HABITATION

Two single people receive more benefit than a married couple. If you are living with your boyfriend or girlfriend you may be assessed as husband and wife. The **Supplement-**

ary Benefits Commission stresses that a decision depends on whether a couple are living together as husband and wife, and not on whether they have on occasion slept together. But individual officers are given a large amount of leeway in their decisions.

## OTHER BENEFITS

People in receipt of Supplementary Benefits are automatically entitled to free dental and medical treatment, free school meals for children, milk and vitamins for under 5's and various other benefits. You should be given information on all such benefits by Social Security. An excellent booklet on citizens rights and welfare benefits is available from the Social Work Department, 14 Castle Terrace, Edinburgh.

## FAMILY INCOME SUPPLEMENT

Family Income Supplement is a con designed to keep wages down and favour employers rather than recipients. Those eligible are families where the head is in full time work (i.e. over 30 hours a week) and has one or more children. It is designed supposedly to bring an inadequate income up to a government determined minimum income level, and is based on the number of children in your family and on a certain scale of minimum income levels.

Those eligible for F.I.S. and Social Security are also eligible for the welfare benefits mentioned under 'Other Benefits' above. Full details and an application form are obtainable from any post office on leaflet F.1S.1. If your income falls below the under-mentioned levels and you have the appropriate number of children, you'll be entitled to half the difference between your income and the government-determined level.

| No. of Children | Govt. qualifying income level |
|---|---|
| 1 | £21.00 |
| 2 | £23.50 |
| 3 | £26.00 |
| 4 | £28.50 |

and £2.00 for each additional child. For example, if you earn £15.50 a week and have 2 kids, you qualify for a Family Income Supplement of £4.00 a week.

The maximum you can receive under this scheme if £5.00. It is normally payable for 26 weeks at a time, after which a renewed application will be necessary. When you apply you should also send your payslips for the previous 5 weeks (2 months if you're on a salary).

## VOLUNTARY SERVICES

There is a plethora of voluntary bodies varying from large organisations to small groups run by the old dear down the road. A complete list of these can be found in the "Directory of Social Services in Edinburgh" from the **Edinburgh Council of Social Services,** or bookshops. Here is a short list of bodies to contact for help:

**EDINBURGH COUNCIL OF SOCIAL SERVICES, AINSLIE HOUSE, 11 ST. COLME STREET,** (225 4606) co-ordinates voluntary and unpaid social work in the city. Its activities range from Schools Action Edinburgh to chores for the old and disabled.

**CITIZENS RIGHTS OFFICE, 11 CASTLE STREET** (226 6347) run by Scottish Poverty Action Group gives advice and assistance in claiming the various social security benefits and in appealing at Welfare Benefit Tribunals. Open Mon., Wed., Fri. 17.00—20.00 Tues. & Thurs. 14.00—17.00.

**CITIZENS ADVICE BUREAU, 58 DUNDAS STREET** (556 6179/ 5039) are good for legal and complainants' advice and used to dealing with bureaucratic hassles.

**SHELTER HOUSING AID CENTRE, 8 FREDERICK STREET** (225 6058) open 9.30 — 17.30 weekdays. Helps families (individuals who are homeless or have housing problems. Aid and advice given free on problems in general relating to housing.

**RENT REGISTRATION SERVICE, 6 COATES CRESCENT** (225 5534) Statutory but nevertheless useful, deals with enquiries about the legal aspects of renting furnished or unfurnished accommodattion. Application forms for a rent reduction can be obtained here.

**CRAIGMILLAR HEALTH WELFARE AND ADVICE CENTRE, 182 GREENDYKES ROAD,** (669 1257) run under Government Auspices and designed as an all purpose community aid centre covering everything from medical problems to free legal advice.

**COMMUNITY ACTION GROUPS/TENANTS ASSOCIATIONS** do not always have a very long life. To find out if there is an association in your area contact **JIM SMITH** of the **EDINBURGH TENANTS CO-ORDINATING COMMITTEE 31/4 WEST GRANTON LOAN 9552 7582).** They can be useful pressure groups.

Even if you don't need help, get involved in any of these groups or contact **ENTERPRISE YOUTH, 29 QUEEN STREET** (226 3192/ 6412). Community work, at best, can be a direct stimulus to political action.

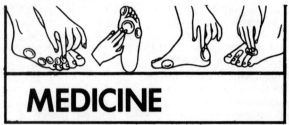

# MEDICINE

Medical treatment is provided under the NHS, the only charge being 20p per subscription. You can claim exemption from these charges if pregnant, if receiving supplementary benefits and for children under 15 and people over 65. For information ask at your doctor's, chemist or Social Security office. Foreigners are treated free, but only for illnesses originating in this country.

## DOCTORS

A list of general practitioners can be found in the telephone directory and since most operate an appointments system, phone first. Most chemists can dispense a doctor's prescription, and are open late by rotation (the nearest late shop is advertised in the window of any chemist). The best is Boots Shandwick Place, closing at 21.00 every weekday. In the case of a late night emergency, not requiring emergency admission to hospital, your G.P. will treat you.

Remember if you are not satisfied with the treatment from your general practitioner you are entitled to transfer to another G.P.'s list in your area.

## EMERGENCIES

Phone your own doctor — if you haven't got one, phone the police who will put you in touch. In a serious emergency e.g. road accidents, self-poisoning, dial 999 and call an ambulance. Many hospitals provide 24-hour casualty services.

ROYAL INFIRMARY OF EDINBURGH, 1 LAURISTON PLACE. (229 2477). Deals with all emergencies for adults, including drug overdoses.

**WESTERN GENERAL HOSPITAL, GRIEVE ROAD. (332 1311).** Has a modern casualty department that at present is not so overloaded as the Royal Infirmary.

**LEITH HOSPITAL** has a casualty department available 24—hours but cannot deal with all emergencies — try one of the others if you can.

**ROYAL HOSPITAL FOR SICK CHILDREN, 9 SCIENNES ROAD. (667 6811).** Deals with children only.

**PRINCESS ALEXANDRA EYE PAVILION, CHALMERS STREET,** has a 24—hour emergency service for eye injuries.

## DENTISTS

For residents dental treatment is paid for, half by the patient and half by the NHS, up to a maximum of £10. The charges for visitors vary from one dentist to another, so check first. Some dentists have long waiting lists, often up to months. However, free but only temporary emergency treatment can be arranged at the Dental Hospital, 32, Chamber's Street. (225 5261) open Mon. — Fri. 9.00 — 10.30 and 14.00 — 15.00 (except August). Only real emergencies are treated on Saturdays, 9.00 — 10.30.

## VENEREAL DISEASE (V.D.)

The venereal diseases are a group of infections which are transmitted by sexual intercourse. They take their name from Venus, the Goddess of Love. In Great Britain the venereal diseases were defined by Act of Parliament in 1916 as syphilis (pox), Gonorrhoea (clap) and a rare tropical disease known as chancroid, but since then the term V.D. has been used to encompass all sexually transmitted diseases such as Trichomoniasis, (a protozoal infection) Candidiasis (yeast infection), Pediculosis pubis (infestation by the crab louse) and Scabies (or 'itch'). V.D. is common, but it is important if you think you have it to get treatment not only for your own sake, but also for your partner's(s') . Some of the diseases, after the initial symptoms have subsided, if untreated can lead to serious complications (e.g. heart disease and insanity from syphilis or permanent sterility in women from gonorrhoea.)

The main symptoms in men are: sores on the penis, pain on urination and a discharge from the penis; and in women, vaginal discharge, itching, pain on urination, upset periods, sores around the genital area and pain on intercourse. However, there may not be any obvious symptoms at all. For example, 30 per cent of women infected with gonorrhoea are entirely symptomless. Gonorrhoea involving the rectum occuring in women and homosexual men may also produce no symptoms for a long time.

Confidential treatment can be obtained either at your G.P. or at the V.D. Clinic of the Royal Infirmary, Lauriston Place, Edinburgh. (031-229 2477):

Men: Ward 45 (phone extension 108); Women: 46 (phone extension 109) — both in the Skin Block at the Tollcross end of the Infirmary.

Open:  9 am — 12.30 pm Mon.—Fri. (males and females).
       9 am — 12 noon Sat. (males and females).
       4 pm — 6.30 pm Tues. and Fri. (males only).
       4 pm — 6.30 pm Mon. and Thurs. (females only).

An appointment should be made by phone if possible. Privacy is guaranteed.

## CONTRACEPTION

Male contraception — conception can be prevented by the use of a sheath or condom which is worn on the penis during intercourse to trap the seminal fluid. They are freely available from chemists, hairdressers and from dispensing machines in many gents toilets in pubs and hotels, in packets of 3 for about 20p or by post at about half price, e.g. Family Planning Association, 27/35 Mortimer St., London, W.1. (01-636-7866). This method is easy to use and relatively safe, although slight leakage from an imperfect product or bursting of the condom may occur, or they can slip off altogether; risk can be minimised by the use of a vaginal spermicidal cream, foam or pessary in addition to the condom. One disadvantage is the interference with sensation to both partners.

Coitus interruptus or withdrawal just before ejaculation is a bad method for both partners psychologically and is not very reliable as it is wholly dependent on timing and control by the man.

Female contraception — contraceptives such as the Pill, the Coil or Loop and the Cap or Diaphragm, are only available through a doctor or clinic. Any doctor is able to prescribe them but not all do. At present, expect to pay for the contraceptives, unless they are prescribed for a medical condition. However, Parliament is in the process of considering proposals for the incorporation of Family Planning into the National Health Service and contraceptives may then be available free on prescription.

There are two clinics in Edinburgh that provide contraceptives:

**THE BROOK ADVISORY CENTRE, 2 LOWER GILMORE PLACE.** (229 5320 Mon. — Fri. 9.30 pm — 2.30 pm and 7.30 pm — 10.30 pm) now offers contraceptive advice, abortion counselling, pregnancy testing and advice on sexual or emotional problems. A clinic especially for the unmarried or unsupported. Edinburgh residents should soon be able to use the service free, but those from outside Edinburgh are charged a fee of £4 for a year's care. They will take the payment by instalments to make things easier and never turn away anyone who is genuinely unable to pay.

**THE EDINBURGH FAMILY PLANNING CENTRE, 18 DEAN TERRACE, EDINBURGH, EH4 1NW** (332 7941). (also at Clermiston, Gilmerton, Greendykes, Lochend, Prestonfield, Sighthill and West Pilton. For details phone 332 7941). Provides contraceptive advice to anyone over 16 years. The service is free to Edinburgh residents. Others pay a consultation fee of £4. Free supplies for medical cases (maybe all family planning will soon be free). Vasectomy sessions. Appointments are necessary either by writing or phoning. Mon. — Fri. 9.30 — 17.00, and Mon. — Thurs. 18.00 — 20.30.

## PREGNANCY TESTING

Your doctor can do this free. The Family Planning Centre charges £1 if you are a patient, £2 if not. The Brook Advisory Centre charges £1. Take along a sample of urine (taken first thing in the morning) in a clean bottle. The tests are usually accurate 10 days after the first missed period.

Alternatively you can send a sample of urine to a commercial testing service which costs about £3. A local one is Newington Laboratories Pregnancy Testing, 37 Clerk Street, Edinburgh 9. (667 7534). Or, you can obtain 'Do-it-yourself-kits' costing about £2—3 from some chemists. If you want to be really sure, go to a doctor.

## ABORTION

The Abortion Act 1967 made termination of pregnancy a legitimate procedure in certain specified circumstances. Most, but not all, doctors in Edinburgh are sympathetic towards abortion. If yours is not, he must refer you to another who is. Unfortunately this does not always happen. Even if you are refused an abortion by a consultant gynaecologist you have the right to ask for a second opinion. Termination is desirable before the end of the twelfth week, as it can then be undertaken by the vaginal route and the time required under medical supervision is only 24 or 48 hours.

Services exist to put you in touch with sympathetic doctors:

THE BROOK ADVISORY CENTRE, 2 LOWER GILMORE PLACE. HELP! INFORMATION SERVICE (554 6908)

BRITISH PREGNANCY ADVISORY SERVICE, GUILDHALL BUILDINGS, NAVIGATION STREET, BIRMINGHAM, B24 BT. (02-643 1461). A non-profit-making registered charitable trust. Patients referred for termination of pregnancy to their own and other nursing homes. Can cost about £41 for B.P.A.S. nursing home and £65—95 for other private nursing homes. Consultation fee £10.

## PSYCHIATRY

Psychiatric treatment under NHS is free but you must be referred by another doctor. Psychiatric problems are very common, but often your general practitioner can treat your illness without referral to a psychiatrist. Non-NHS psychiatric treatment was provided by lay-analysts at the Davidson Clinic which has now closed down, but HELP (554 6908) can refer you to one if desired. Fees are of the order of 2 gns. a session. HELP is interested in establishing a branch of People Not Psychiatry (P.N.P.) an organisation in London that provides an alternative to the usual psychiatric treatment available. Anyone interested in forming a P.N.P. group should contact HELP.

MOUND CENTRE, 52 QUEEN STREET (225 6028), which deals largely with alcoholics, gamblers and drug addicts.

SAMARITANS, (225 3333), prefer to work by phone and provide a sympathetic ear for anybody who is really down, but they can also get in touch with lawyers and doctors to give professional advice if it is needed.

## ADOPTION

Those placing a child for adoption and those applying to adopt are advised to apply to a registered adoption society. The services below also offer help to the unmarried mother in keeping the child.

THE SCOTTISH COUNCIL FOR THE UNMARRIED MOTHER AND CHILD, 44 ALBANY STREET. (031-556 3899).

GUILD OF SERVICE, 21 CASTLE STREET (031-225 6441).

## ALCOHOL

Alcoholism is the biggest drug problem in Edinburgh. It was estimated recently that one family in ten in Scotland has a member who is an alcoholic. Most people are already aware of the physical and mental effects of alcohol. Withdrawal symptons are essentially the same as for barbiturates (see Drugs Section.) For further details on the misery of alcohol addiction the reader is referred to a paperback Pelican by Kessel and Walton entitled 'Alcoholism.' Different forms of treatment are available from:

THE ALCOHOLISM UNIT OF THE ROYAL EDINBURGH HOSPITAL, MORNINGSIDE PLACE (447 2071). Normally you have to be referred by a G.P. for treatment.

EDINBURGH AND DISTRICT COUNCIL ON ALCOHOLISM, 27 CASTLE STREET, (225 4519) provides a counselling and advice service and can put you in contact with people who'll help.

ALCOHOLICS ANONYMOUS, SIMPSON HOUSE, 52 QUEEN ST' (225 6028) holds group meetings in various parts of Edinburgh. Phone or call for details.

## DRUGS

A drug is defined by the Interim Report of the Canadian Government Commission of Inquiry as "any substance that by its chemical nature alters the structure or function in the living organism." This includes anything from nicotine, alcohol and caffeine that are socially acceptable in our society to cannabis, opiates, etc. Drugs have their uses and abuses like anything else that intrigues man.

The following notes are on the commoner illegal drugs encountered on the Edinburgh drug scene. They are by no means comprehensive, and for those that are interested, a selection of the better books on drugs can be found in Better Books, Forrest Road.

**Cannabis** (pot, shit, grass, marijuana, dope.) — Cannabis sativa is a variety of hemp plant which exudes a resin containing tetrahydro cannabinol (THC) a hallucinogen. Cannabis produces two distinct varieties: marijuana, (or grass) consists of the dried flowering tops of the female plants mixed with crushed leaves and twigs, and may vary considerably in potency from one sample to another. The majority of grass in Britain comes from South West Africa and less frequently from E. Africa and S.E. Asia. The second and far more common cannabis product in Edinburgh is Hashish (shit) the concentrated resin produced by the flowers of the female plant. In approximate order of potency (although the best grade of Moroccan is far superior to the worst grade of Nepalese) hash comes from Nepal, Afghanistan, Pakistan, Lebanon, Turkey and Morocco.

It's effects, depending of course upon quality and quantity, mode of ingestion, etc. last between one and five hours. The "high feeling" is basically an increased awareness of one's surroundings, resulting in the intensification of various aspects of the world around; colours seem brighter, music more intense, new patterns emerge in normally trivial objects and so on. Inhibitions are lessened though a strong dose especially taken orally can induce paranoia — everyone is staring at you, no-one really likes you, etc. — which will be over as soon as the peak of the dose has passed, and rarely reaches the intensity of a bad trip. Physically there is a dryness of the mouth and lethargy.

The eyes become reddened but contrary to popular belief there is little evidence of pupil dilation. Less commonly, nausea, vomitting, diarrhoea or constipation occurs. Appetite is generally increased. At high doses in some individuals inco-ordination, staggering and tremors have been noted. Hangover effects even after high doses are rare. There is little reliable information of the long-term effects of cannabis use, but its major disadvantage is its illegality despite several recent reports that the penalties for possession of cannabis should be reduced. (The Wooton Report for Great Britain 1968. The Canadian Commission of Inquiry into the Non-Medical Use of Drugs 1970, Mr.

Nixon's Commission of Inquiry 1972).

L.S.D. (acid or lysergic acid diethylamide) — the "problem solving psychedelic", is a supremely potent drug. A mere 20 microgrammes (millionth of a gram) will have an effect and an average popular dose is between 200 and 500 microgrammes.

It is sold in a wide variety of forms. Originally one took a sugarcube onto which an indeterminate amount of acid had been dropped. This has been largely superceded by tablet and capsule forms, the former tending to be stronger as it is more difficult to tamper with the dose. There is also blotting paper acid, microdots and gelatin squares, all of which come in a variety of hues and 'brand' names (strawberry fields, white light, etc.)

Acid is sometimes cut with speed (amphetamines), strychnine (a stimulant at low doses, but also a deadly poison), atropine or barbiturates to intensify or prolong the experience. (One sample of mescalin seized by the Edinburgh Drug Squad was found to contain L.S.D. and barbiturates. The chances of obtaining pure mescalin are very slim in this country.) Sometimes, but rarely, L.S.D. tabs contain other synthetic hallucinogenic drugs such as M.D.A., S.T.P. (Serenity, Tranquility, Peace), D.M.T. or P.C.P. (angel dust, phencyclidine, an animal tranquilliser.)

The content of an L.S.D. trip varies from person to person and depends to a considerable degree on various personality factors, past history and experiences, attitudes, expectations, the general setting in which the drug is taken, person's accompanying the 'trip' and external events accompanying the experience. Taken orally the effects usually occur within an hour and the major effects last 8—12 hours. Physical effects can include nausea and vomiting, increased heart rate, dilation of the pupils and headaches which occur in the early stages of a trip. The subjective effects are infinitely varied. Visual and aural hallucinations, merging of the senses, (synesthesia) so that sounds are 'seen' and colours are 'heard', a breakdown of established time reality so that seconds may last for eternities, feelings of insight and lucid thoughts occur, degrees of depersonalisation, varying from a feeling of 'spaced out' of communication with other people all the way to a merging of oneself ('oneness') with the world.

Bum trips — There is no guarantee no matter how many times you have dropped acid that you won't go on a bummer. With a bad trip a person may experience varying degrees of tension, anxiety and fear, unpleasant illusions, depression and despair. The more serious cases are termed 'freak-outs' or psychotic reactions in which the subject experiences nightmarish terror and panic. Often the bum tripper feels he is going permanently insane or is going to die. While an experienced 'guide' can often help prevent such reactions this is no guarantee against an unpleasant experience.

If a friend goes on a bummer the best way to deal with it is to try and talk him down. Constant reassurance that the tripper is not going insane is essential. Ken Kesey developed a technique called "Total Attention" where the tripper's unpleasant thought stream is diverted onto pleasant aspects of tripping, which are deliberately kept as light as possible. Vitamin C is claimed to be successful in bum trips, but in practise drinking concentrated orange juice often just makes the person vomit. Niacinamide (nicotinamide) Vitamin B and certain tranquillisers are also useful in reducing the effects of a bum trip. Chlorpromajine, a major tranquilliser in rare instances can potentiate the effects.

HELP (554 5908) will come out to anyone on a bummer any time.

The other drawback to L.S.D., apart from its illegality, is the possibility of flashbacks. These are a recurrance of certain aspects of an L.S.D. trip which usually last a few minutes or less. They have been reported to occur even more than a year after the last (or only) trip. Drugs such as cannabis or an emotional experience paralleling some part of a previous trip can trigger a flashback or they can occur spontaneously. This aspect of L.S.D. has worried both proponents and opponents of acid and the best thing to do in such a situation is treat it as you would a bad trip.

Speed — Speed is a generic term for various pills which

are combined under the name Amphetamines. They are in many ways similar to the body's own adrenalin in effects. It is important to distinguish between oral and intravenous use.

The commonly abused amphetamines taken orally include Dexedrine (Dexies — a slimming pill), Drinamyl (Purple Hearts or Blues — a combination of amphetamine type stimulant and central nervous system depressant) and Benzedrine (Bennies).

At moderate doses taken orally there is usually an increased wakefulness, feeling of clearer thinking, an elevation of mood and increased verbal and behavoural activity. The main problem of the milder versions of speed is their ability to cause disastrous self-delusion. There is nothing more tedious than the speed freak rapping incessantly and irrelevantly to a roomful of people who really would rather he or they were elsewhere. Speed, contrary to opinion, is not a good idea to drop before an exam — the work of genius you think you are producing usually turns out to be total rubbish. After continued use of moderate doses, recovery may be associated with tiredness, drowsiness and not infrequently, emotional depression. At higher doses of speed, delirium, panic, aggression, psychosis and hallucinations can occur. The amphetamine toxic psychosis may be indistinguishable from schizophrenia.

Methedrine is the speed that does the killing as it can be used intravenously. Cases are frequent of people attempting to inject other crushed up amphetamines and literally clogging up their veins. Arms swell up and extreme pain is experienced.

The chronic 'speed freak' is a sorry sight. Continued use of massive I.V. doses as tolerance is acquired often leads to considerable weight loss, sores and non-healing ulcers chronic chest infections, liver disease and so on. A further complication is serum hepatitis caused by the use of unsterile injections. This is the picture that people are referring to when they say 'Speed Kills'.

Barbiturates (Downer's) — have a remarkably similar effect to that of alcohol; in fact it is difficult to separate the two subjectively. For pure danger, in the form of overdoses and a high potential for dependence, downers leave mainlined speed or even heroin standing. In addition they are very easy to obtain.

Physical dependence develops, at the same time as tolerance and sudden deprivation of barbiturates (or alcohol) can lead to severe and even fatal withdrawal symptoms, even including nausea, vomiting, tremors, abdominal cramps. epileptic seizures, delusions and hallucinations. With moderate use the effects of withdrawal are considerably less severe.

Some of the commoner barbiturates available are Tuinal (a mixture of Seconal and Amytal) which is a short-to-medium acting downer and Nembutal (nambies, nemmies) which is a short acting barbiturate. Other sedatives are often taken interchangably with barbiturates, tranquillisers such as Valium, and Librium and sleeping tablets such as Mandrax (Mandies.).

Overdoses of barbiturates are common and very dangerous. Alcohol markedly potentiates the effects of barbiturates and they should never be taken in combination. The same applies to Mandrax — Hendrix died that way.

TREATMENT OF OVERDOSES

Best action is to get the person to hospital despite tricky questions. Take any remaining tablets or the empty bottle with you to hospital so that the doctors can identify the drug. If the person is still conscious try and get him to vomit by inserting the fingers into the back of the throat or by giving a drink of salt water, and keep them awake as long as possible. If the person is unconscious, lay them in a semi-prone position to avoid the risk of inhalation of vomit.

DRUG ADDICTION

Registered addicts can obtain supplies under the NHS as an in-patient at the Royal Edinburgh Hospital, but you must be referred by a doctor. HELP (554 6908) can also arrange admission and will try and assist an addict once he is discharged from hospital. HELP can also provide confidential information and advice on any other drugs problem.

Members of the jury, don't hold it against the accused that he is a long-haired anarchist anti-social yobbo nor that he is plainly guilty. Just consider the facts of the case and don't let any bias enter into your decision.

# THE LAW..........

Most of us at some time in our lives will come in contact with the legal system, and yet most are unaware of our basic legal rights. The establishment thrives on our ignorance, so be well armed: read on.

### LEGAL ADVICE & REPRESENTATION

If you feel you need legal advice, or have to appear in Court don't be afraid to consult a lawyer for legal advice. This is advisable even if you intend to defend yourself in Court. The Legal Advice and Assistance Act 1972 which came into force on April 1973 states that a solicitor may give £25 worth of advice to a client for free if his disposable income is under £11 per week or if on National Assistance or Supplementary Benefit. If your weekly disposable income is over £11 but under £20 there is a sliding-scale for contributions, but you'll never have to pay over 48% of the cost of advice.

The Legal Advice and Assistance Scheme does not generally cover representation in Court, this comes under the old Legal Aid Scheme. If, however, you are refused Legal Aid in Court you should go and see a solicitor under the Advice and Assistance Scheme.

## LEGAL DISPENSARIES

CITIZENS ADVICE BUREAU. 58 DUNDAS STREET (556 6179 or 556 5039) Hours: 9.30 — 16.30 Mon.—Fri.; 18.30 — 20.00 Thurs. A centre of valuable free information and advice on anything from legal aid and landlord/tenant difficulties to consumer, hire purchase and personal problems.
Branch Offices: 53 CONSTITUTION STREET, LEITH (554 8144) Hours: 10.00 — 13.00 Mon.—Fri.

CRAIGMILLAR HEALTH, WELFARE AND ADVICE CENTRE. 182 GREENDYKES ROAD (669 1257) Hours: 9.30 — 13.00 and 14.00 — 16.30 Mon.—Fri.

THE NEIGHBOURHOOD LEGAL CENTRE, (same address as the Craigmillar Health, Welfare and Advice Centre, see above) holds sessions every Thursday 18.00 — 20.00. Six lawyers are on hand to give advice. They can dictate letters, not write them or refer clients to social workers or legal aid lawyers. A real attempt to take usually remote legal advice to where its needed.

THERE ARE ALSO SIMILAR CENTRES AT:
GILMERTON, Tuesdays, 18.00 — 19.30 pm
PENNYWELL, Tuesdays, 18.00 — 19.30 pm.

LEGAL DISPENSARY, OLD QUAD, SOUTH BRIDGE. Wednesdays 18.30 onwards. 4 solicitors on hand. They cannot represent clients but can write solicitor's letters and offer free legal advice in an informal setting.

SCOTTISH COUNCIL FOR CIVIL LIBERTIES, (S.C.C.L.) contact David Christie, 6 Strathearn Place, Edinburgh, 9, 447 4410, or 214 Clyde Street, Glasgow, 041-771 7600.

LEGAL AID CENTRAL COMMITTEE, LAW SOCIETY OF SCOTLAND, 27 DRUMSHEUGH GARDENS (226 7411) open until 17.00

## ALTERNATIVE HELP AGENCIES

HELP INFORMATION SERVICE (554 6908) can put you in contact with a number of sympathetic lawyers for legal advice. Provides immediate legal representation for drug busts, etc.
UP AGAINST THE LAW, 1 ELGIN AVENUE LONDON, W.9 (01 289 3881). Is a magazine by and for criminals, defendants, radical lawyers and people like us who have been "up against the law", who are pissed off with the farce of British 'justice', and who are trying to break down the passive role of defendant, and create a few "offendants(!)"

BIT, 146 GREAT WESTERN ROAD, LONDON, W.11.(01-229-8219). A 24-hour a day, 7 days a week information and help service.

RELEASE, 1 ELGIN AVENUE, LONDON, W.9. (01-289-1123). Emergency 24-hour number: 01-289 8654. Provides help with drug busts, legal advice, etc.

## PRESSURE GROUPS FOR PRISON REFORM

HOWARD LEAGUE FOR PENAL REFORM, 17 WARRISTON CRESCENT, EDINBURGH, EH3 5LB, 031-556 1687. Exist to promote constructive penal policies with emphasis on rehabilitation and treatment in the broadest sense.

P.R.O.P. (PRESERVATION OF THE RIGHTS OF PRISONERS) 63 ALBANY STREET, HULL, 0482 223409. Demand a number of rights for prisoners - right to vote, Trade Union membership conjugal rights, etc.

R.A.P. (RADICAL ALTERNATIVE TO PRISON), 104 NEWGATE STREET, LONDON, E.C.1. Research, advocate and campaign for rational and humane alternatives to prison, with a view to eventual abolishment of imprisonment.

## CIVIL RIGHTS

It is also helpful to know what rights you're guaranteed under law. The theory behind the British Constitution is that you are free unless the law says otherwise, but there are so many laws negating this that the constitution is of little importance. Moreover, police in Edinburgh have more powers under local orders than anywhere else in the country. If you feel like sounding off in public, you need no permission to speak at the Mound on Sundays: elsewhere its still legal to speak in public but you may be held responsible for gathering a crowd and threatened with an obstruction charge. The police, of course, are politically prejudiced in the use of the Order of which another part forbids the distribution of any other sort of leaflet but those relating to political matters or to trade disputes within the city. No action is taken against people distributing leaflets for a jumble sale or military tattoo but a Hare Krishna member distributing leaflets which talk about pacifism is arrested. (At the time of press this is likely to be repealed as from August 1973). However, the following description of rights regarding arrest procedure is unaffected by the Order unless otherwise stated.

## PRE ARREST

You are not compelled to accompany a police officer to the station unless you have been arrested. If in doubt ask formally whether you are being arrested — if you are you should be given a reason. Remain silent. THIS IS IMPORTANT. You must give the police your full name and address, but do not make any statement even if you think this might help your case. Innocent sounding statements can be detrimental when quoted out of context in different tones of voice by the prosecution at a trial. You don't have to answer any questions and you are not compelled to have your fingerprints taken unless you've been arrested.

Under the Dangerous Drugs Act a police officer may search you if he has reasonable grounds for suspecting you to be in possession of dangerous drugs as specified in the Act. This means the possibility of search without arrest, and refusal constitutes an offence. You can insist on being searched on the spot (unless this would constitute indecent exposure). A woman can only be searched by a policewoman. The officer must say what he is searching for and under which Act, but if he finds anything incriminating on you, even though it is not what he was originally looking for, it may still be used as evidence against you on a different charge, though this is left up to the Court's discretion and evidence may be deemed inadmissable.

In Edinburgh the possibility of search without arrest also exists under the Edinburgh Corporation (1967) Order which gives the police the right to search a person for stolen property, firearms and game in addition to drugs. (The powers of arrest without warrant for any offence are listed under ss. 446—486).

## ARREST

If anything incriminating is found on you, you may be arrested and taken to a police station. You have no right to know what your actual charge may be but you are entitled to know what the reasons for arrest are. At the station you may be searched again and further items removed as evidence. Once again you are under no obligation to reply to a caution or charge; it is always better to say nothing until you see a solicitor.

The Police must allow you to intimate your arrest to a solicitor. Generally the police phone for you; it is only with their permission that you may phone personally. They must allow a private interview with your solicitor before your Court appearance. HELP (554 6908) and S.C.C.L. (447 4410) can both supply you with a list of solicitors on request. The police must also make 'reasonable' arrangements for your comfort and refreshment, and any property taken from you must be packaged in your presence. Don't sign for anything which doesn't belong to you.

You may be fingerprinted, searched and photographed (all records should, of course, be destroyed if you are acquitted) but not compelled to answer any questions. The police may try to obtain further information by offering inducements such as 'making it easy for you'. Beware of the 'nasty' policeman leaving you alone with the 'nice, friendly one' who 'will see to it that you get off lightly if you help them with any further information'. They cannot honour these agreements as all prosecutions are made by the Procurator Fiscal. Always remain polite and reasonable, however, and secure the presence of an independent witness wherever possible. (If bust with a friend, ask for him to be present at all possible times).

## COURT

If charged do not offer any plea until you have obtained legal advice — if in doubt plead not guilty. You may decide to change your plea later when you've seen a solicitor — this will not prejudice your case. Remember you may think you're guilty but legal advice may show otherwise.

You are entitled to a private interview with a solicitor before your hearing. HELP Information Service can arrange immediate legal representation at the police station and in Court if they hear of anyone being arrested for large quantities of drugs. If not there is always a legal aid solicitor on duty at the Court to advise you. If

163

the police offer no objections bail will be granted. The usual objections are; likelihood to abscond (no fixed address and unemployed); the seriousness of the offence; and the presence or absence of a previous history of abusing bail. If bail is refused for any reason a solicitor will visit anyone remanded in custody.

If you are refused legal aid — this happens occasionally especially if faced with an offence under the Dangerous Drugs Act, "if you can afford to buy drugs you can afford a solicitor" obtain free advice under the Legal Advice and Assistance Act 1972 from a solicitor on how best to handle the case. At the Court hearing take along a friend to advise, and assist you when you defend yourself — a 'McKenzie Man'. HELP and S.C.C.L. should be able to help you with this.

Anyone can stand bail if they have the money. This is recoverable at the end of the trial (with interest after 31 days in the bank.) Cheques are not normally accepted except from solicitors.


## SENTENCE

If you're found guilty the minimum sentence will be an absolute discharge in which case stand still and take it. In order of severity this is followed by admonition, suspended sentence, and probation.

For fines, ask for time to pay. Probation means visiting some overworked, underpaid guy with good intentions so don't take it out on him.

Prison is a badly organised system of human degradation both for prisoners and prison officer — you'll need all your personal strength and the help of good friends to keep its effects to a minimum. Find out all you can about your privileges, especially on remand in custody like visitors passes, food parcels, books, magazines and meals and wine brought into you, and exert them to the fullest extent.

The Scottish verdict of not proven is an historical accident which means they think you're guilty but can't prove it. This cynical verdict has the same effect as not guilty or an acquittal.

## COMPLAINTS

Since it is the ardent admirer of the police who investigates complaints, most of the cases (surprise, surprise) end up being labelled 'unsubstantiated' and not brought to trial. In 1970 there were over 10,000 complaints against the police; 90% ended up buried. In the past 5 years the police have been the subject of over 50,000 complaints. 5,577 of those were so blatant that they couldn't be covered up and were reluctantly stamped 'substantiated'. This reflects only the number of people who have actually gone to all the trouble of formally making out a complaint. Most people usually don't bother particularly when the charges are serious since all they will probably get as a result, is harassment by the police, and they know that unless they happen to be blue-nose members of the establishment, nothing will come out of the police's investigation. Only 10 policemen in Scotland have been charged following complaints in the last few years and none in Edinburgh.

For "non criminal" complaints for instance, about police conduct, write a letter to the Chief Constable. If he decides to take action, and the decisions rest solely on him, he will ask for an interview with you. You may ask for it to take place in a solicitor's office. At the disciplinary hearing which is the next step, you have no locus standi — i.e. you have the right to be present only when giving evidence.

For criminal complaints the best action is to address complaints to both the Chief Constable and the Procurator Fiscal at the same time, as soon as possible after the alleged offence.

## SQUATTING

It is a criminal offence in Scotland unlike England. Police can evict you under 1865 Trespass Act.

## OBSCENITY

Charges under the Edinburgh Corporation Order 1967. This order makes sellers of articles which are "liable to deprave or corrupt" punishable by a maximum of £50 fine or 60 days in jail.

Defendents may plead in their defence that they were ignorant of the contents of an obscene article. On the other hand under the order literary merit is no defence.

Most defendants plead guilty. They would be ineligible for legal aid as they would appear in the Burgh Court and the cost of a lawyer would probably be greater than the cost of a fine if pleading guilty.

There has been a spate of obscenity busts in the past year. Student, Better Books, Cracker and raids on head shops — used to be only the hard core porn merchants (about 10 convictions per year of stag party films, bookshops, etc.)

## DRUGS AND THE LAW

The Misuse of Drugs Act 1971 supercedes the previous fragmentary drugs legislation. Drugs are classified into 3 categories.

Class A: Heroin, Methadone, Morphine, Cocaine, Pethidine, mescaline, L.S.D., Opium.

Class B: Codeine, Dihydrocodeine (DF 118), Amphetamine, Dexamphetamine, Methylamphetamine, Cannabis and cannabis resin.

Class C: Berryphetamine, Mandrax.

Types of offences included under the Act are:

1. Importation or exportation.
2. Production.
3. Cultivation.
4. Supply.
5. Possession.
6. Allowing the premises to be used for certain illegal purposes.
7. Frequenting a place used for the purpose of opium smoking.

The maximum sentence for an offence for Class A and B drugs, except for possession, is 14 years or an unlimited fine or both. For possession the maximum sentences are:

Class A: 7 years or unlimited fine or both

Class B: 5 years or unlimited fine or both

Class C: 2 years maximum sentence.

For the benefit of the average smoker it should be pointed out, however, that for a normal case of possession of a Class B drug, this will be dealt with by summary proceedings (before a judge and without a jury) where the maximum sentence is limited to 6 months or a £400 fine or both.

## POLICE ORGANIZATION IN EDINBURGH

For administrative purposes, the police force in Edinburgh is divided into six divisions: four area divisions, A-D, which police various parts of the city; E division which is the Traffic Department; and H.Q. which includes the C.I.D. and various specialised departments. Since the introduction of the Unit Beat Policing (the system of 'panda' car patrols), district police stations now have a complement of a detective sergeant and constables, although most of the C.I.D. still operate from Police Headquarters. The unit beat policing system now covers 89% of the City's area and 70% of the population. The City centre continues to be policed by traditional means.

## HOW TO FIND THE POLICE

SOUTH SIDE POLICE STATION, CAUSEWAYSIDE — DIVISIONAL H.Q. 'A' Division. 031 667 3361
District Stations:
Craigmillar District Station, Niddrie Mains Rd., 031 661 3362
Mayfield District Station, Mayfield Road, 9, 031 667 7272
GAYFIELD SQUARE, just off LEITH WALK, H.Q. 'B' Division 031 556 2011
District Stations:
Drylaw District Police Station, Ferry Road, 4., 031 332 2258
WEST END POLICE STATION, TORPHICHEN PLACE, near HAYMARKET — 'C' Division H.Q. 031 229 2323
District Stations:
Corstorphine District Station, Meadowplace Rd., 12. 031 334 4900
Oxgangs District Police Station, Oxgangs Rd. Nth. 13. 031 441 1518
LEITH POLICE STATION, QUEEN CHARLOTTE ST., 6. at foot of LEITH WALK — 'D' Division H.Q. 031 554 1212
District Stations:
Portobello District Office, High Street, 15. Tel: 031-669 1638
Traffic Wardens Department, Lothian Road, 1. 031 22°
Wireless Station, Blackford Hill, 9. 031 447 626⁷

POLICE HEADQUARTERS, HIGH STREET, 031 225 1212, main entrance in Parliament Square: for most problems, especially to get permission for anything, like a demo, ask for the Chief Constable's Department. For licences of any kind, ask for the Licensing Department. Also based at H.Q. are the C.I.D., the Traffic Department, Court Department, Operations Room and the Central Charge Office, and the Lost and Found Department. Round the corner in the High Street itself is the Aliens Department, with Aliens, Firearms and Dangerous Drugs Sections.

DANGEROUS DRUGS SQUAD:— the squad works in "close liaison" with the C.I.D., not only making busts but also accumulating information. It consists of four operational officers, with recourse to officers from other departments when needed. They do not make a distinction between pushing and using, the charge of illegal possession being uniform; they leave it up to the Courts to take this into account. If sufficient evidence is available the alternative charge of supplying or attempting to supply illegal drugs can be applied. According to Inspector Rogers of the Squad, "Every regular drug taker is a pusher. They are all pushing on a small scale". (The incidence of illegal drug usage in Edinburgh is almost certainly on the increase. The number of busts has certainly increased, and one may be sure that the majority of cases never reach the attention of the police).

CRIMINAL INVESTIGATION DEPARTMENT:— Based mainly at H.Q. but each area division has a detective branch under a Detective Chief Inspector. Has various specialised branches to call upon, including the Identification Branch for forensic work (sometimes helped by the two universities here) and the Criminal Records Office. There is also the Fraud Squad for large-scale commercial crimes, the Murder Squad, and the Flying Squad which "concentrates on the movements and activities of the criminal fraternity". The Criminal Intelligence branch has as its function "to obtain, evaluate, collate, record and disseminate current information concerning the movements, habits, associates and intentions of the criminal fraternity".

# COMMUNICATIONS

Communication is what its all about really. Almost by definition the alternative, or libertarian, community is splintered into small groups which direct their energy against the aspects of the establishment each finds most oppressive. There is a need to communicate between these groups — from technical help and advice, sharing equipment disseminating news of what is happening to particular groups which will affect the interests of them all, to co-ordinating direct help in an emergency. It is also essential to be able to communicate ideas, attitudes and information from these groups to the world at large. This kind of dissemination may be done directly through handouts, posters or through alternative publications — but has inevitably only local effect. There are, of course, the national media — over whose editorial policy and manipulation of your ideas and efforts you can have no control.

Its important to be able to get wide coverage of your campaign, demonstration, event, etc., but you should not be surprised at the distortions which emerge after being processed through the capitalist press.

This section provides addresses at which to contact straight local and underground news sources and might conceivably help you in producing your own newspaper, poster or broadsheet.

## EDINBURGH COMMUNITY

As with most local communications media, those in Edinburgh are long in potential but short in support, money and practical help. Many people project Cracker, Roots and Student Publications Board into being dillentantist cliques without ever getting close enough to find the truth for themselves. This attitude which may come from a mixture of insecurity, ignorance and resentment of someone else who is actually doing something, is encouraged by a similar attitude in the people who are involved in these groups. But help is needed and will be accepted gratefully if it's offered openly. There is usually no money in writing for the local press but you do have the chance to have a direct influence on the development of its potential.

One of the most encouraging developments in Edinburgh since last year has been the establishment of HELP, as an information and assistance clearing house. As usual it was formed on the initiative of a small group of people but that doesn't mean they want to keep it exclusive.

CRACKER, 5 SPITTAL ST. (229 6291). Newspaper and entertainment guide. Always needs sellers, journalists, artists etc. 7p fortnightly.

EDINBURGH UNIVERSITY STUDENT PUBLICATIONS, 1 BUCCLEUCH PL. (667 5718 or 667 9278). Publishes Alterhative Edinburgh, Student, New Edinburgh Review, among others. Always open to ideas and needs sellers, writers, artists.

HERIOT-WATT STUDENT PUBLICATIONS, 30 GRINDLAY ST. (229 3574) publishes Omega fortnightly during termtime.

ROOTS (is moving premises, phone messages taken by HELP). gives info on diverse subjects relating to Edinburgh and non-violence also contains short stories, poetry and funnies. Monthly-6 weekly 8p.

HELP (554 6908) Info./Aid Service. Will provide: 24 hour advice on legal representation for drug busts, etc., crash pads, medical advice, drug problems, and information on a large number of other subjects and organisations.

## UNDERGROUND PRESS & INFORMATION

To say the least, 1973 has been a bad year for the underground newspaper — with the demise of OZ, Spike, Frendz, Fapto , Black Box and Agit Prop.

The trend is to emphasise the importance of the community and to support activities at a local level. National underground papers never achieved financial viability, or a sufficiently efficient organisation to survive on their news content. Those which have survived push the comix, rock music and drugs angle — which has a limited variety and limited appeal. The function of co-ordinating underground news dissemination is being taken over by agencies—like Quest and the Peoples' News Service.

QUEST NEWS SERVICE, ROOM 209, 2 VICTORIA STREET, LONDON, SW1 OLD. 01-222 7456. Info service on social matters in Britain. Monthly bulletin.

PEOPLES NEWS SERVICE, 149 CLAPHAM ROAD, LONDON SW9 Tel: 01-735 2088. Weekly news bulletin of social and political conflicts in Britain.

BIT, 146 GREAT WESTERN ROAD, LONDON W.11. 01-229 8219. 24-hour info/help service. Publishes Bitman, an info and news bulletin.

TOUCH, PEDDIE STREET, DUNDEE. (Being squatters they move around a bit but can be contacted by writing to or going to Peddie Street).

ART & COMMUNITY WORKSHOP & CLAIMANTS UNION, 6b POWIS CIRCLE, ABERDEEN(0224 491570).

U.P.S. (Underground Press Syndicate), P.O. BOX 82, HEAD POST OFFICE, BATH. A persistent attempt to form an underground news agency which aims to ensure that important stories get national coverage by syndication of copyright among its members. Subscriber newspapers pay a small membership fee.

RISING FREE, 197 KINGS CROSS ROAD, LONDON, W.C.1. 01-837 0182. Took over from Agit Prop as a political info service and distributor for conventional and libertarian political publications. They have a mail order service. Send a SAE for a list.

SMOOTHIE, 67 VERE ROAD, BRIGHTON. Publishes 'Contacts' — a list of alternative help and info centres throughout Britain, and the 'Directory of Alternative Media Publications'.

The remaining nationally distributed underground press comprises:

GAY NEWS, 34d REDCLIFFE SQUARE, LONDON. SW10. Tel: 01-373 0586. Fortnightly newspaper for homosexual men and women.

IT, 116 WARDOUR MEWS, LONDON, W.1. Tel: 01-437 1312/ 434 1372. The oldest underground paper in Europe, now fortnightly, 15p and guarantees a regular total change of identity.
ROLLING STONE, 28 NEWMAN STREET, LONDON, W.1. Tel: 01-580 6045. Basically an American rock music paper but branching out into social and political commentary. 20p fortnightly.
PEACE NEWS, 5 CALEDONIAN ROAD, LONDON, N.1. Tel: 01-837 9794/5. Weekly, aspiring to non-violent revolution. 7p.

## THE STRAIGHT PRESS

Well, they have big circulations and insatiable appetites for copy. Its not too difficult to get coverage of your campaign or event. You may have to decide whether creating a newsworthy angle to your activity compromises its validity in any way. Most alternative groups prefer to have as much coverage as possible — but it is a conflict which shouldn't be dismissed lightly.

Its also worth getting to know a few journalists with whom you can exchange information. They often have knowledge, or even stories, which they can't use for various reasons — lack of popular appeal, too politically loaded or potentially libelous. Journalists, in their turn, are desperate for new sources of views and ideas.

To drum up press coverage phone their number (reversing the charges) and ask to be put through to the newsdesk. You can do this before or after whatever you're doing. It's also theoretically possible to ring up, ask for copy and then dictate at slightly slower than normal speed a report that you have written. This way you go straight to the subeditors and do not have to go through a reporter. It would obviously be a help if you can speak direct to a journalist you know — who might take more of an interest in what you are saying and could have more sway in seeing that its used.

Biggest selling dailies in Scotland are the 'Scottish Daily Express', selling near to 600,000 at the last count, and the 'Daily Record' (over 540,000). Edinburgh's only national daily, 'The Scotsman', has a Scottish circulation of 76,000. All the big dailies, however, have Scottish branches —
DAILY RECORD, & SUNDAY MAIL, 30 FREDERICK ST., EDINBURGH 2. (225 4275).

DAILY TELEGRAPH, WITHY GROVE, MANCHESTER (061-834 1234).

EVENING NEWS, 20 NORTH BRIDGE, EDINBURGH (225 2468).

GLASGOW HERALD, 5 SOUTH ST., ANDREW ST., EDINBURGH (556 7421).

THE GUARDIAN, 22 FLESHMARKET CLOSE, EDINBURGH, 1. (226 6508).

THE SCOTSMAN, 20 NORTH BRIDGE, EDINBURGH (225 2468).

SCOTTISH DAILY EXPRESS & SUNDAY EXPRESS, 61 JEFFERY STREET, EDINBURGH, 1. (556 3933).

THE TIMES, 56 HANOVER STREET, EDINBURGH, 2. (225 — 6875).

In addition, the United News Service, 22 Fleshmarket Close (225 — 8271) is a good straight news agency, covering stories for The Times, Daily Telegraph, Guardian, Daily Mail, Glasgow's Evening News and Evening Citizen, and Dundee's Courier and Evening Telegraph.

## PRODUCE YOUR OWN PAPER

The first problem is money. If you get over that problem then you can start worrying about luxuries like content, distribution, ideology, design and direction.

With the cost of paper and labour continuing to rise it's a very rare newspaper that can stay solvent through sales alone. That would require a high circulation and a high price per copy. Most publications eventually get round to touting for advertising which implies a deliberate ideological decision. Difficulties inevitably arise over whether to refuse certain advertisers and to resist the temptation to alter the content to suit the advertisers rather than the producer.

It is often possible to apply for a subsidy from the Scottish Arts Council or another benevolent foundation. The same conflict tends to arise in that anyone who gives you money is liable to want to 'guide' what you are producing. The Arts Council also demands a high percentage per issue of original literary work — which rules out most political publications.

It's important to have an idea what kind of market you're producing your publication for. Most underground papers preach their message largely to the converted. If you can find a way of making your publication attractive to a wider public, without diluting the content, then you shouldn't miss. Time Out achieved financial solvency on a large scale — and found that in itself brought problems.

## PRINTING

In this area there is no community owned printing works, half tone camera or even duplicating machine. Therefore, even though you do your own typing and layout you still have to pay a professional to do the actual printing. A group called the Aberdeen People's Press were recently given £750, part of a legacy left to BIT to distribute to good, alternative causes. They have bought the equipment for their own press and workshop — which is available to all left-wing, community and alternative groups in Scotland. The idea is that you should learn to use the equipment yourself — and avoid having to take your business to a professional. They can be contacted at:—

ABERDEEN PEOPLES PRESS, 10 RUBISLAW DEN SOUTH, ABERDEEN, AB2 6BB.

If you can't get to Aberdeen then the following printers are cheapish and not too interested in the political nature of what they print:—

PORT SETON OFFSET PRINTERS LTD., COCKENZIE, 7094 559.

CENTRAL PRINTING COMPANY, 69 CUMBERLAND ST., EDIN. 556 2183.

24-HOUR PRINTERS, 58A GEORGE ST., EDIN. 2. 226 3468.

METRO PRESS, 12A MANOR PLACE, 226 7157.

If none of these is satisfactory to you try these firms, further afield.

MOSS SIDE PRESS LTD., MANCHESTER (061 226 3458).

PRINT AND PAPER, 90 PAISLEY ROAD WEST, GLASGOW. (041 427 1253).

ANDREW SINGER, WHOLE EARTH TOOLS, THE MILL COTT—AGE, SWAFFAM ROAD, BOTTISHAM, CAMBRIDGE.

For lists of small presses and advice on setting up your own, contact the 'Association of Little Presses', 262 Randolf Ave., London W.9. (01-624 8565).

## DUPLICATING

A useful process for small newsheets. Most large organisations, including trade unions, have duplicating equipment, so use your contacts there. If you're a student or have friends who are, get the student union or SRC to do them for you (Edinburgh University charges 40p for 50 copies). The various office services in the city are more expensive, charging anything from £1 to £2 for the first 100 copies (prices reduced for each subsequent hundred)— 'ABC' in Coates Crescent are good here. Don't bother buying your own duplicator unless you'll be using it full-time.

For equipment literally all that is needed to start with is a room, telephone, table, chair and typewriter — later you can aim for a lay-out board or light-box. For typewriter sale or hire, see the yellow pages. (Edinburgh Office Supplies, 72 Haymarket,) sells second-hand manual typewriters, £25-£70 while electric models go for anything from £65 to £120). If you're hiring typewriters it's cheaper to rent by the month (average £8 a month for manual and £17 for electric). Simpson Bell, Hanover Street, gives a good deal here. Start off a filing system immediately, using cardboard and wooden boxes if necessary. A list of printers and news contacts will also be useful, and you can build up a basic reference library from review copies, swopping newspapers, etc.

You don't need professional help if you have a reliable team and you're willing to learn. Everyone on the staff should be acquainted with the law as it affects press and printing, and at least one person with experience of printing techniques is valuable. Editorial decision-making is important: theoretically, this is best done by continual discussion and consensus among the team but the faster — and more limited — way is to have strong central direction. Don't let this mean one person is left to do the lot. No matter which you choose, it's important to give time regularly to communal discussion and ideas. Other problems to be solved are those of advertising and publicity and sales. For distribution of local or community newspapers, there's no need to go through the chain organisations, which inevitably demand too big a cut — deal directly with independent shops wherever possible, as well as concentrate on street, pub and door to door sales.

## STREET TRADING

To sell anything in the streets of Edinburgh a licence is

required; to sell anything, that is, except newspapers and periodicals. For a publication to classify as such it must be published regularly, e.g. a monthly would count as a periodical whereas an annual or bi-annual would not. If in any doubt check with the Town Clerk's office at the City Chambers or with the Chief Constable's Department, at Police Headquarters. If a stall or similar device is to be used, then a licence is needed even for periodicals.

To apply for a Street-trading licence, ask for an application form at the Town Clerk's office. The application should take about three weeks' to go through, and the licence will be valid until 28th May and costs £2.

### REGISTRATION AS A NEWSPAPER

To make sure of the cheaper postal rates for newspapers, it is necessary to register with the GPO as a newspaper This costs £1 per year, and written application must be made to the Head Postmaster, Edinburgh (there is no application form) together with a copy of the publication. The paper should contain at least one-third news and be published at least once every seven days. The name of the paper should appear on each page with the date. If the paper is finally registered with the GPO, the fact must be mentioned in each edition.

## MASS MEDIA

### LOCAL RADIO

Edinburgh will not have a local BBC Station but an IBA commercial station is imminent and should be in operation in 1974. This is our one big chance to influence the local media. The time is ripe for real community radio and already one group is working along these lines. Anyone interested should contact RADIO EDINBURGH (229 9651).

Community Radio gives us the choice to make 'mass media' into 'mass communication' again, with real community involvement in programming and the widespread use of 'phone in' and 'access' type programmes can make radio exciting and alive again. Do it now!

## TV & RADIO

Start a write-in campaign to press for an Alternative News Programme similar to that broadcast by BBC Radio London and put together by BIT. Till that happens use the existing mass media to the full. Here's a list of News & Current Affairs programmes to contact:

BBC: 12 noon, Radio 4, weekdays. Contact John Gray or Michael Shaw, BBC, 5 Queen St., Edinburgh (225 3131).
BBC 1 TV: 'Reporting Scotland'around 18.00, contact Donald Munro, BBC, 5 Queen St. (225 3131).
BBC Northbeat: 17.30 weekdays, Radio 4, contact BBC Aberdeen, Beachgrove Terr., Aberdeen (0224 2533).
STV: News and Current Affairs, contact Gateway Theatre, Leith Walk, Edin. 7 (556 5372) or Theatre Royal, Hope St., Glasgow (041 332 9999)—Bob Cuddihy.

## ALTERNATIVE MEDIA

Guerilla Radio is practical and cheap. The simplest and quickest way to get on the air is to modify an amateur or ex-army transmitter for broadcast use. The CODAR RADIO CO LTD. markets an 80/160 meter band called the A.T. 5 (see ads in monthly mags) which can be easily adapted to service a housing estate. Here's a list of pirate radio stations available in the Edinburgh area—all are members of the Scottish Free Radio Movement:

CAROLINE SCOTLAND, 222 metres, Sunday afternoons.
RADIO FREE CAROLINE, 229 metres, Sunday afternoons.
CHANNEL, 225 metres, weekends.
CAROLINE SOUTH, 217 metres, Sunday afternoons.
CAROLINE INTERNATIONAL, 262 metres, Sunday afternoons.
RADIO OZ, projected, Sunday afternoons.

Perhaps the most exciting new media development is V.T.R. or video equipment. Anyone interested should contact Jules Warren, c/o Pilton Tenants Association, who is experimenting with video in Pilton.

# SPORT

For sport freaks here's a list of activities to give your body some shape!

**SPECTATOR SPORTS.** Watch Hearts and Hibs play on alternate Sats. 15.00 Aug-April at Tynecastle Park (Gorgie Rd.) and Easter Road (off Leith Walk) respectively. Free visits can be arranged. So phone grounds!

Watch out for sporting events; e.g. championship athletics, cycling held at Meadowbank Stadium; Edinburgh Highland Games annually in mid August); East of Scotland tennis championship at Craiglockhart, and New Year professional sprint at Powderhall; motor-racing at Ingliston; speedway at Coatbridge; horse racing at Musselburgh, dogs at Powderhall. Some way out activities there!

## Outdoor

Football—from professional First Division to a kick-about on wasteground—dwarves the Edinburgh sports scene, but side by side almost unnoticed there has grown up a myriad of varied recreations—skiing, orienteering, kart racing, even hot air ballooning—many sponsored by the Corporation. Below is a guide to the best non-snobbish and cheapest ways of taking part.

**RUGBY:** Join a club. Contact District Secretary Mr. I. Morrison, 46 Elliot Road (441 2921).

**HOCKEY:** Men—try Inverleith Club; HQ at Thistle Tennis Club, Craiglockhart. Women—try Edinburgh Ladies, Frogston Road. Contact Pat Blain (556 2840).

**TENNIS:** Either join a club or use Corporation courts, e.g. Meadows, (off Melville Drive); Regent Road; Leith Links; and Inverleith. Tops are those at Craiglockhart.

**GOLF:** Public courses are:

Braids 1 & 2, Braid Hills. Fast greens. Rough.

Carricknowe, Balgreens Road. Long and flat.
Silverknowes, Silverknowes Pk.
Craigentinny, Craigentinny Avenue. Closed '72.
Portobellow, Stanley Road. 9-hole. Half price.

BOWLING: All happens at Meadows East and West, Regent Road, Princes Street, Iona Street.

SKIING: Zoom down to Hillend (No. 4 bus). Hire equipment too! Open all year round.

MOTORING: Truck on over to

Edinburgh and District Motor Club Ltd. Club premises, 28 Nelson Street (556 1031).

Edinburgh Southern Motor Club, Secretary T. Robertson Pendreigh Avenue, Bonnyrigg, Midlothian (663 1518).

Edinburgh St. George Motor Club, Secretary Mrs. Anderson, 12 Marchmont Road (229 4068).

Melville Motor Club, Secretary T. Hay, 64 Salvesen Gardens, (556 2129).

WATER SPORTS: Swim out-of-doors at Cramond Beach and Portobello Beach. Far out! (so might the sea bed). Portobello pool is open air (09.00-21.00 in summer months). Fishing TROUT: Colinton Dell, St. Bernards Wall, Powderhall at Water of Leith. SAITH: Newhaven Harbour by the Lighthouse; COD: Musselburgh Lagoons.


**Indoor**

Tops is Meadowbank Stadium, London Road. (No. 4 bus) with amazing range of facilities. It's not cheap, so become a member. However, indoor sports are covered by the Corporation and community centres.

SWIMMING: Commonwealth Pool, Dalkeith Road (3, 33, 47). Opens 09.00-22.00, and 08.00-20.00 Saturday and Sunday. Separarate Adult's and Children's pools.

Dalry, Caledonian Crescent (midday to 20.15).
Glenogle, Glenogle Road (midday to 20.15).
Infirmary Street (off the Bridges). 09.00-19.25.
Leith, Junction Place (09.00-19.25).
Portobello, Bellefield Street (09.00-20.25). Open air (June to September.)
Warrender, Thirlestane Road (midday to 19.25). Aerotone and Turkish baths.

BADMINTON: Well sponsored by the Corporation. Run from Sept. to June at Schools and community centres. Here is a list.

Leith Community Centre (Wed.) New Kirkgate.
Royal High School (Mon/Wed/Thur). Regent Road.
Gracemount School (Wed/Thur), Lasswade Road.
St. Thomas (Thur), Chalmers Street.
James Gillespies (Mon/Tues), Marchmont
Bruntsfield (Tue/Wed), Montpelier Park
Firrhill (Mon-Wed), Firrhill.

KEEP FIT: Most Corporation centres have keep fit centres. Check out possibilities with the Corporation's Guide to Recreation and Leisure Activities" available from Adult Education Dept. St. Giles Street. The centres are:

Leith, New Kirkgate, Large sports hall.
Pentlands Youth Centre (serves Oxgangs, Firrhill and Colinton. 25p family membership with other charges.
Pilton Community Centre, Pilton Drive North.
Sighthill Youth and Community Centre, Sighthill.
Northfield and Willowbrae Community Centre, Northfield Rd.
Inch House Centre, Inch Park, Gilmerton Road.
Pentland Youth and Community Centre, Oxgangs Brae.

# ESCAPING
# ESCAPIN
# ESCAPI
# ESCAP
# ESCA
# ESC
# ES
# E

## ESCAPING WITHIN THE CITY

When the city encroaches on your sanity and you really have to get away there are lots of places, even within the metropolis. If all you need is mild therapy, try the city's parks:

**ROYAL BOTANICAL GARDENS:** Take a trip to the 'Botanics'; walk back by Inverleith Park and Pond.

**CALTON HILL:** Good views but tends to emphasise the urban environment rather than help you escape.

**CRAMOND TO GRANTON:** Walk along the esplanade, 155 acres of grass, but avoid weekend rush.

**MEADOWS:** Just about big enough to forget the city; good lunch-time escape.

**SAUGHTON PARK:** Possibly best kept formal gardens in Edinburgh.

Alternatively, try a peaceful town walk

**DEAN VILLAGE:** Old Mill Village of Edinburgh; walk under Telford's Dean Bridge to Stockbridge; don't miss Ann St., possibly the most beautiful Georgian street in Edinburgh.

For other walks, useful books are city transport's 'Walks

181

from City Bus Routes' and 'Edinburgh for Children'.

Country walks within the city — even our own 'mountain'

**ARTHUR'S SEAT:** nearest thing to fresh air in Edinburgh — lots of routes — from Duddingston Loch to Dunsapie and then to the Summit; from Pollock Halls up Radical Rd. (built by the unemployed at ½d per day in the 1840's) and down to St. Margaret's Loch; from Holyrood up Haggis Knowe up the side of Hunter's Bog to the Summit, etc. etc. Arthur's Seat is an old volcano 823 ft. high. Stoned views of the city at dusk or dawn.

**BLACKFORD HILL AND POND:** Walk up from Blackford Hill to the Observatory; pick brambles in the autumn. Alternatively, through Hermitage of Braid (rhododendrons in spring).

**CORSTORPHINE HILL:** Lots of wooded walks on top of the old RSG 6, nuclear hideout for the elite until exposed by the Committee of 100 a fews years ago.

**SWANSTON TO HILLEND:** Reach Swanston off Oxgangs Rd. then over Lothianburn golf course to Hillend ski slope; for more adventurous walks in the Pentlands, see our next section.

The City's Town Planning Department have drawn up proposals to create 60 miles of walkways along the city's abandoned railway lines and canals.

The plans include walkways along the entire Water of Leith along the Union Canal, another along the Niddrie burn and along Slateford/Balerno railway line.

So why not use them now? Well, strictly speaking it's illegal and the police occasionally prosecute, but most are already well established walks (e.g. Slateford/Balerno, etc.) and our phantom tresspasser's favourite walk is the railway line which runs in a straight line from Canonmills to the Old Union Pier Bar, ideal on balmy evenings. For more ideas just look at any Edinburgh Map.

## ESCAPING FOR THE DAY

If you've exhausted the Edinburgh escapes or if you need the real thing, go to the country.

**CRAMMOND TO S. QUEENSFERRY:** a favourite walk. Take ferry (2½p) from Crammond Village across the Almond and follow the coast through Dalmeny Estate. See how the aristocracy live and find super beaches and picnic spots. Stop for a pint in Queensferry; if more energy, walk over the Forth Road Bridge.

**THE PENTLANDS:** Chairlift to the top of Hillend then follow Peaks to Bavelaw and Balerno. A702 to Flotterstone, then via Glencorse to Balerno. A702 to Carlops and walk via Bore Stane to A70 then Balerno. A702 to W. Linton, then follow old drove road up valley of N. Esk to A70 Lanark Road.

**ROSLIN TO LASSWADE:** At Roslin, see beautiful chapel with intricate carving; then take path to Roslin Castle and the Esk. Follow winding river through Gorge to Lasswade.

**DOLLAR TO DOLLARBEG AND GLENDEVON:** From Dollar walk up river valley to Dollarbeg Castle with great views, then either return by gorge or continue over hills to Glendevon — Youth Hostel, pub and Hotel.

**BEACHES: TANTALLON:** Continue on A198 past N. Berwick and past Tantallon Castle and take cart track at second right angle bend past castle. Fabulous, as yet unspoilt, beach below cliffs of Castle, unique, tiny harbour carved out of the rock.

**TOWNS:** If you can take towns, Fife is scattered with attractive hamlets. Explore Culross, St. Monance, Pittenweem, Anstruther and Crail.

**LOCHS:** Loch Leven makes up most of the county of Kinross. It is famous for trout and the castle where Mary Queen of Scots was imprisoned.

**RESERVOIRS:** Visit Edinburgh's reservoirs and see just how short of water we are. Threipmuir and Harperrig are both worth a visit and Tala off the A701 at Tweedsmuir is really spectacular with a 1 in 5 gradient road leading over to St. Mary's Loch and then by B709 to Innerleithen.

**HILLS:** Try Innerleithen to Middleton or Stow (B709).

# COMPLETE ESCAPE

If you've plenty of time, take the A90 to Perth then A93 to Blairgowrie, Glen Shee, Braemar and Aberdeen. Then slow down and follow the coast. Some nice places to camp or visit —

LITTLE FERRY, near Golspie, miles of sandy beach.

TALMINE, at the end of a tiny road on the Kyle of Tongue.

CAPE WRATH. Most northerly point on G.B. mainland.

The most beautiful and spectacular scenery in Scotland is between Ullapool and Skye — don't leave without seeing it even if it costs you money. Stoned sunsets at Gairloch with only the Atlantic between you and America will make it all worthwhile.

Explore it yourself but don't miss —

FALLS OF MEASACH, in Corrie Shalloch Gorge nr. Ullapool.

LOCH MAREE, Applecross Peninsular, Plocton.

Camping on the west coast —

SHEIGRA — sand and peace.

CRUINARD BAY — sand and sea.

OPPOSITE LONGA ISLAND NR. GAIRLOCH is one of the most beautiful campsites in Scotland. Alternatively south of Gairloch take B8056 to Red Point. You can camp almost anywhere but ask farmer. In bad weather YHA are cheapest but restrictive (list from SYHA, 1 Warrender Park Rd.). Great alternative hostel at Glen Cottage, Glen Torridon, 25p a night, run by 2 folk singers.

SKYE: If you go to Skye visit Elgol and also Sleat Peninsular, don't miss Kylerhea ferry — like something in Shangri-la.

COMING BACK: If you're coming back to civilisation take A87 to Inverary then A82 through Great Glen, Glen Coe and south via either Loch Lomond and Glasgow or Loch Earn and Callander.

## GOING TO THE COUNTRY

Look out the window, what do I see?
cows hangin' out under spreading trees
ZOOM! they're gone behind the sign
white letters pointing to the long white line
and I'm going to the country
o, la la la la la
I'm going to the country
sunshine smile on me

I can smell the grass growing in the field
wind in my hair tells me how it feels
farm house, silver roof flashing by
tractor-trailer truck says goodbye with a sigh
and I'm going to the country
o, la la la la la
I'm going to the country
sunshine smile on me

birds singing, I'm singing in my bones
doesn't much matter now where I'm going
get it when I get there is what I'll do
if I get enough I'll give some to you
and I'm going to the country
o, happy as can be
I'm going to the country
sunshine smile on me

Bruce Cockburn
Bytown Music Ltd.

## HOW TO GO

Hitching in Scotland is easy but don't waste time hitching in the city or walking to the outskirts. Use buses to get to prime hitching points.

Once in the lift be pleasant to the driver and he will stop for other people. Remember cars are faster than trucks. Single males are best for lifts, couples stop only occasionally and single women or families almost never. Use your hitching energy accordingly.

**GOING SOUTH, by east coast:**
SMT bus from St. Andrews Sq. to Wallyford Roundabout on A1. First target lift at least to Berwick on Tweed.

No. 33, 49 Corporation bus to Cameron Toll Garage A68, first target lift to Dalkeith or preferably Morpeth then A1 south.

**by west route:**
No. 4 Corporation bus from Princes Street to Hillend terminus then A702. First target lift to Abingdon then A74 to Carlisle, M6 south. Wastes between bleached with the bones of many hitchers.

Busier but longer: No. 31 Corporation bus to Maybury roundabout then A8 to Glasgow Road. First target lift Newhouse then to A74 south to Carlisle.

Probably best route A1, habituees may wish to savour different routes, best alternative A68.

**GOING WEST:**
No. 31 bus from Princes Street to Maybury roundabout; A8 to Glasgow and the west.

No. 31 bus from Princes Street to Maybury roundabout; A9 to Falkirk and Stirling then north or west.

**GOING NORTH:**
18/41 or 20 bus from Charlotte Sq. to Barnton roundabout then A90. First target lift at least to Forth Bridge, preferably to Perth then north to Inverness or n/e towards Aberdeen or Dundee.

No. 31 bus Princes Street to Maybury roundabout then Stirling, Callander, Fort William.

Other routes out of Edinburgh are possible but quiet and not recommended.

## CHEAP TRAVEL

If you decide you want to pay there are bus, train and air services from Edinburgh, but first check out any concessions you can get.

For students there are 2 main agencies: NUS, 12 Dublin St. (556 9954) and BSTC (226 6513), George IV Bridge. NUS trains can be used by all full time students over 14, staff, nurses, teachers, and ex students for two years. Planes for full time students over 16, similarly ships and hovercraft, have flights almost anywhere in the world, nice people; BSTC concessions are only available to full time students, at least officially. At their best on cheap train fares — Edinburgh/London £4.85.

Alternative to BSTC and NUS Travel —

Brian Hughes,
196 High Street, Billericay, Essex.
— offers student air charters/trains/boats with a longer summer season than usual with student travel, also permits recently lapsed students to use their service.

(For other cheap travel fares see Exchange & Mart, Private Eye, IT, Time Out, etc.).

## STRAIGHT TRANSPORT

BUSES: Eastern Scottish Bus Group area covers the south east of Scotland from its main Bus Station at St. Andrews Sq. and with other services links all parts of Scotland. They also have tours, package holidays, private hire and parcel services. Prices are usually slightly cheaper mile for mile than rail. Buses are at their best for short journeys. The overnight direct London service is popular because at £3.25 it is the cheapest way between the cities, but the 11-hour trip is exhausting and not to be recommended unless you love buses and motorway cafe food.

Full information on services from 556 8231 (when not engaged). Also sell a timetable price 3p, including a map of SE Scotland — good value.

RAIL: Stations; Waverley and Haymarket, Waverley main station. For information phone 556 2394. Current best deal — London, return for £7.90 if you book 21 days in advance. Also check out cheap day return fares, and Runabout rover tickets (NB Area 8).

FLIGHTS: There are no direct international flights from Turnhouse. The main operators are BEA and British Caledonian, BEA have flights to Aberdeen, Barra, Benbecular, Campbeltown, Glasgow, Inverness, Islay, Jersey/Guernsey (in summer), Orkney, Shetland, Stornoway, Tiree, Wick and London (Heathrow) with connections for international flights. British Caledonian offer an alternative connection to London via Gatwick. Cut price offers are constantly changing. For current information on cheapest fares — standby, under 21, student, excursion, etc. phone:

BEA, 225 2525

British Caledonian, 225 5162

Any other enquiries: Turnhouse, 334 2351. Cheapest way to get to Turnhouse — SMT buses 42, 43, 44, 32 from St. Andrews Sq. every half-hour.

# ALTERNATIVE

# FUTURE ?

to be governed is to be
WATCHED OVER
INSPECTED
LEGISLATED AT SPIED UPON
REGULATED DIRECTED
PREACHED AT DOCKETED
CONTROLLED
CENSORED INDOCTRINATED
ORDERED ABOUT ASSESSED
WEIGHED
by men who have neither
the RIGHT nor the KNOWLEDGE nor the VIRTUE
to be governed means to be
at each operation
at each transaction
at each movement
NOTED CONTROLLED STAMPED
registered taxed measured
VALUED PATENTED AUTHORISED
assessed licensed endorsed
ADMONISHED REFORMED ARRESTED
hampered rebuked

Bureaucracy is the work which most characterises 20th-century life. It worms its way into every nook and cranny of our existence. At every turn we are confronted with the faceless, depersonalised "homo bureaucratis".

The time is ripe to reverse the trend and give Edinburgh back to its people. People before rules, people before profits, people before cars, Homes before offices.

Of course it's pure idealism to suppose this guide will change any reader's attitude. Or that even if it changes all readers' attitudes, that this is all it would take to create an Alternative Culture in Edinburgh.

Basically we've got to deal with the series of paradoxes and contrasts that shape the city's life: the arty/cultural image when in fact the city is neither liberated nor permissive; the fostering of old and historical Edinburgh for tourists when in fact there is little council interest in preservation and false economies are continually made to keep the city rates low; the image of the people's city centre which in fact is being rapidly depopulated for hotels, offices and university expansion.

At present changes are directed by the whim of the investor or developer, like the recent St. James Square complex off Princes St., or by ad hoc responses to crises. From now on people and not profits should decide planning decisions.

Direct action is what Edinburgh needs most now. Bur information is the beginning of understanding, and our book tries to supply the info on what is going on and the beginnings of ways to liberate ourselves.

It may be that Hugh McDiarmid was right when he wrote:

"Talking with five thousand people in Edinburgh yesterday
I was appalled at their lack of love for each other,
At their lack of ecstasy at the astounding miracle
Of being alive in the flesh and together with one another,
And amazed that men and women each superficially so
        different
Should be so obviously the product of the same
        temperament,
Dyed in the same vat to a uniform hue."

We—the people trying to live our lives in this city—have endured too much negativity and false tradition and have every right to echo McDiarmid's cynical conclusion—

"It's far too late in the day
    for a fellow like this
Trying to organise a conspiracy of feelings
    in Edinburgh of all places".

But we're trying to explode the old echo with a new shout.

Join us!

You know it makes sense!

# INDEX

191

CLOTHES, JEWELLERY, RECORDS, JEANS, THINGS

21 COCKBURN ST.
up from Tourist Office